Set Free Childhood

Parents' survival guide
to coping with
computers and TV

Martin Large

Illustrated by Kate Sheppard

Hawthorn Press

Published by Hawthorn Press, Hawthorn House, 1 Lansdown Lane, Stroud, Gloucestershire, GL5 1BJ, UK
Tel: (01453) 757040 Fax: (01453) 751138
E-mail info@hawthornpress.com
Website www.hawthornpress.com

Drawings and cover illustration © Kate Sheppard
Cover design by Hawthorn Press, Stroud, Gloucestershire
Typesetting by Bookcraft Ltd, Stroud, Gloucestershire
Printed by The Cromwell Press, Trowbridge, Wiltshire
Printed on acid-free paper from managed forests

British Library Cataloguing in Publication Data applied for

ISBN 1903458 43 9

Contents

Acknowledgements

Many thanks to a whole range of people who have helped with information and support, including: John Travers, Fenya Hancock, Ewout van-Manen, Faith Hall, Roald Dahl, Sally Jenkinson, Christopher Clouder, Susan Linn, Joan Almon, Lars Maren, Hans Sand, Jane Healy, Dave Grossman, Tim Coombs, Alex Murrell, John Gush, Aonghus Gordon, Mario Peters, David Hubbard, Keith Buzzell, Dorothy Singer, Jane Gerhard, Daniel Large, Judy Large, Nathan Large, Emily Fridenskold, Russell Evans and many others.

Especial thanks to the Hawthorn Press team of Rachel Jenkins, Managing Editor, Frances Fineran, Design, Lynda McGill, Sales and Alan Lord, Finance and especially the Early Years Series Editor, Richard House, for his thorough editing, feedback and support.

List of terms

ADD	Attention Deficit Disorder
ADHD	Attention Deficit Hyperactivity Disorder
CCTV	closed-circuit television
CRT	cathode-ray tube
EEG	electroencephalogram
EMR	electromagnetic radiation
ICT	information and computer technology
IT	information technology
RAS	Reticular Activating System
RSI	repetitive strain injury
VCR	video recorder
VDT/VDU	visual display terminal/visual display unit

Foreword

'TV rots your brain.' So spoke my 6-year-old nephew when explaining why he had hidden his grandfather's remote control for the TV. The same sentiment was expressed by a 6 year old in my kindergarten when a friend asked why he had no television. They were a generation apart but had come to the same conclusion. With a touch of pessimism, one might comment that nothing much has changed regarding children and television over the past 30 years.

A few things have, in fact, changed – but they work in opposite directions. On the one side, children in the United States sit in front of screens for more hours than ever before when you add together time spent with television, films, and computers. This means they are more sedentary and more obese, and as a result suffer from Type 2 diabetes in alarming numbers – a disorder which used to be called 'late-onset diabetes', an affliction of sedentary 60 year olds. Now it is growing at epidemic rates among children and teens.

On the other side, there is more awareness than before that screen time is unhealthy for children – not just physically unhealthy but also socially unhealthy. It interferes with children's desire to move and be active; but it also diminishes their imagination and creativity. Here in the United States, one sees more and more bumper stickers on cars – always a sign of the direction in which public consciousness is developing – advocating the death of television. 'Kill your TV', some stickers are now saying.

My primary concern about children's exposure to media has to do with the issue of how children grow and develop their full human capacities, and the many ways in which our culture interferes with this. For children to develop well, they need caring adults with whom they have much contact and who inspire them to develop their full range of human abilities – mental, social, emotional, and physical. Even the best of media programs cannot begin to inspire children in the way that a loving adult can. Yet far too often, adults are calling upon the media to baby-sit their children. They often feel guilty about this, for they know that media is no substitute for their own attention and care; but the pressure in their lives leads them to do it anyway. So what is the result?

I began working with young children over 30 years ago as a nursery/kindergarten teacher. When I started, many people said to me, you'll love working with young children. They are so open and imitative. I found this openness to be characteristic of about half of the children – but what about the other half? In varying degrees, they were guarded and closed off; it was hard for them to open themselves to me or to others. For some it was understandable, for their family life was painful and difficult. We were gradually able to help these children feel warm and protected, and they began to open up. But there were others who were an even greater challenge, for there was no obvious reason why it was so difficult to find the real child hidden within, and help him or her to come forth and blossom.

Often these were the children who watched a lot of television. As I became more confident of my diagnosis, I began working with families, one at a time, who were willing to turn off the television and see if it made a difference. Their experiences were astonishing, and the most common remark I heard was, 'I never knew what a wonderful child I had'. In the kindergarten I could usually see the difference within a week, as the 'child within' began to emerge again.

The most striking example was a boy named Tony. He was big for his age and could be quite aggressive with other children. He always seemed to feel under attack, and his play was full of monsters, sharks, and other violent creatures intent on destroying him. No wonder he reacted with aggression! After several conversations with me about the situation, his mother made a great effort and cut back significantly on his viewing time – and almost immediately I could see the difference. His play scenarios became less threatening, and his behavior became more social toward the other children and the adults. Tony was now blossoming. However, he then went away for a week with his mother to visit his grandparents. Like so many Americans, they had the TV on from morning 'til night.

Tony came back to the kindergarten full of fear and aggression. After a week or two he calmed down, but a few months later he again went to see his grandparents for a week. His play again reverted to fearful scenarios. Three times during the year he went to visit his grandparents, and each time the pattern was the same. One could have drawn a graph of his play behavior showing steady gains and deep losses each time he was exposed to so much television.

I believe that Tony is far from being unique. Many children react to screen time just as he did – by becoming more vulnerable and then responding with aggression. Others become more withdrawn and sink into themselves. Screen time affects children differently, and how much each child can handle varies in part in relation to how many other stress factors are present in a child's life. I now think of media viewing, including computer usage, as a stressor in a child's life. A perfectly healthy child can handle a certain amount of stress, but most children today already experience too much stress in their homes, child care programs, or schools. For them, even a small amount of media exposure can be too much.

As I came to see the effects of media viewing in the lives of individual children, I began to wonder how it affects families and society as a whole. I received one insight during a trip to Ecuador where I lived with a wonderful family for a month. Each evening after dinner the whole family gathered in the parents' bedroom, nestled together on the bed and chair, and watched the soaps for an hour. It was characterized by a similar warmth and enjoyment of one another's company that I experienced around their meal table three times a day. Yet I was struck by the fact that they did not look at each other in the way they did over the meal table. Everyone just stared at the screen. I could see the handwriting on the wall. Soon, the college-age sons would want a television in their room, then the teenage daughter, and finally the kindergarten child. The family would then be truly Americanized, which means they would no longer embrace each other but would sit and stare at screens for hours each day. What a loss.

Another insight into how television can impact a whole country came in Tanzania, a beautiful country which I visited for the first time nearly ten years ago. I had worked with Waldorf schools in South Africa and Kenya before, and had fallen in love with Africa and the warmth of African people. In Tanzania, though, there was an added element, and it was hard to put my finger on it. I met many adults on that first trip and nearly always my experience was the same: a few moments of polite reserve while we formed those important first impressions, and then a gentle opening on their part that allowed deep and meaningful human meetings to take place. Many of those meetings still resound in me. They were the sort of meetings that happen here in the States or in Europe on occasion, and which I treasure; but in Tanzania they happened every day, and many times a day. How was this possible?, I wondered. Then I learned that television had only been allowed in the country three years earlier: prior to that, it had been banned. I was meeting adults who had not grown up with television. They were genuine human beings, behaving in a clear, open manner in the way we were meant to be.

I tried to speak to them about the effects of television viewing, especially on their children, but the experience was so new that they could not yet see the downside of it. When I returned a few years later, many parents and teachers began to express their concern, for they could see a growing aggression and violence in their youth and wondered if it was linked to increased television viewing. The answer is almost certainly 'yes', as is evidenced through the research of Dr Brandon Centerwell, an epidemiologist at the University of Washington (and research quoted later in this book). He studied patterns of homicide in the United States, Canada, and South Africa over a 40-year period, and found a clear link between increased television viewing and the growth of violence in a country.[1]

In my bleaker moments I wonder what it will take to wake us all up to the negative effects of media in our lives. It is not that we have to ban it for ever, but rather that we learn to view it like we view alcohol. Some people can handle moderate amounts while others need to stay away completely. No one benefits from large quantities, and addiction is a disaster for the individual, family, and society. Media viewing is the same, yet we train our children to consume large amounts of it with our blessings.

Surely it is time to change our behavior; and it is my great hope that this book will help bring about such changes.

Joan Almon
Coordinator, US Alliance for Childhood

1. Television, Computers, and the Age of E-Overload

Children take their time to grow up. Whilst each child is unique, life's developmental journey – of learning to walk, speak, and think in the first three years, for example – unfolds step by step. But whilst the stages and passages of children's growth and development have remained essentially unchanged for thousands of years, for the first time in human history babies and children are now exposed to the rapid, sometimes frenetic pace of modern technology. Whilst children's needs remain relatively constant and enduring – for example, for loving relationships, good food, time for learning and play, and a calm rhythmical family environment – the world is relentlessly speeding up. The result can be that children simply don't have a childhood any more.

We are seeing babies being 'jump started' with computer software that promises to increase intelligence. Watching the *Teletubbies* is supposed to improve toddlers' language – so we hear choruses of *Uh Oh*'s in the train carriage. TV programmes, already designed to glue young eyes to the tube, give way to interactive computer games which are geared to keeping children on-screen – and with children continually pestering their parents to buy more and more. The electronic media are increasingly used in schools, not just as tools but as replacements for teachers – and the marketers of such companies as Microsoft and MTV claim to 'own children's minds'. At the same time, research shows that the electronic TV/cathode-ray tube medium is uniquely suited to gaining open access to children's minds. And the content, whether it be advertisements or inappropriate programmes, can have a powerful influence on behaviour, as we shall see later in this book.

Take, for example the 6-month-old baby who just couldn't calm down and sleep; or the class of 7 year olds who found it hard to concentrate. The 5 year old who had nightmares and suffered from severe anxiety; and the toddler who could hardly speak except for the words, 'bang, bang!' In all these examples, and as we will see later, when parents and teachers decided to go screen-free, the children soon started to thrive.

However, the pace of electronic media innovation is, if anything, speeding up, as ever more sophisticated TV and computer products are manufactured to engage babies and children, with parents being assured that such programmes as the Teletubbies are entertaining and 'educational'. In fact, there exists to date no hard research evidence to validate what are, surely, highly dubious educational claims made for such children's TV programmes.

One conclusion from all this is that *the needs of young children and the demands of the electronic media are on a collision course ...* and with children and childhood being the losers, in all kinds of ways. The result is an epidemic of learning difficulties, the unleashing of pester power, increased anti-social behaviour, eating problems, sleeplessness, language delay, a general sense of dissatisfaction, and a whole raft of emotional problems.

However, help is at hand to assist parents in countering the effects of the electronic media on their children. The purpose of this book is to analyse the best available research on the hazards of the electronic media, so you can make informed choices about what is best for your child. Whilst I argue from healthy child development principles that before the age of 7, the less the electronic media are used by children, the better, constructive ways of coping with TV and computers will be suggested for the over-7s, so you can then make the best use of them when your children are old enough to benefit. Finally, I will suggest how we can campaign against the flagrant commercialization of childhood which is such a defining feature of modern Western culture.

Many parents are very concerned about the effects of both computer- and TV-induced electronic overload on their children. They are also worried about the effects of the toxic commercial environment, as marketers flood children with advertising, with the single-minded aim of creating and 'capturing' lifelong consumers. The food industry links soft drinks, junk food, and sports drinks to films, video games, videos, toys, and celebrities. There are 'sound pops' or 'hot licks' which are 'interactive candies' that include a lollipop in a battery-operated handle – the lollipop spinning when your 'tongue turns it on'.

The inexorable rise of aggressive marketing targeted at young children over the last ten years has become a public health hazard, according to Susan Linn of Harvard University Medical School. Linn sees a direct link between such marketing phenomena, and the toxic commercial environments they create, on the one hand, and soaring levels of childhood obesity and type–2 diabetes, on the other. Children are certainly being inundated with marketing: in the United States, for example, they see more than 40,000 advertisements per annum on TV alone, with the amount spent on advertising aimed at children increasing from $6.2 billion in 1992 to $12.2 in 1999. Linn points out that 'A pre-schooler's risk of being obese increases for every hour of television watched per day. If there's a TV in his or her bedroom, the odds of being obese jumped an additional 31 per cent for every hour watched.'[1]

One of the major weapons in the marketer's toolkit is that of *pester power* – getting children to nag their parents to buy (which reaches a particular climax in the lead-up to Christmas). However, an increasing number of parents and childcare professionals are actively opposing this 'selling out' of children. For example, at the September 2002 Summit on the Commercialization of Childhood in New York City, Alvin Poussaint of Harvard Medical School's Stop Commercial Exploitation of Children Coalition (SCEC) said of advertising to children that '… the trend is accelerating, and it's time we responded honestly to marketing's impact on our most vulnerable citizens – children'.[2] And Michael Brody of the American Academy of Child and Adolescent Psychiatry said, 'Just like paedophiles, marketers have become child experts.'[3]

This commercial, TV-dominated onslaught on young children is quite unparalleled. However, both parents and educators are increasingly making connections between this noxious commercial environment and recent increases in the incidence of learning difficulties, attention problems, anxiety, sleep difficulties, eating disorders, anti-social behaviour, and language impairment amongst children. As Michael Brody puts it, 'The sick child as viewer/consumer has replaced the healthy child of play, sports, and make-believe.'

So what does all this mean for you and your child? For one mother, it meant that children are growing up reluctant to imagine, and to picture stories for themselves, preferring the mass-produced images of films. She was asked by a young child what she thought of the Harry Potter film, so she replied that she hadn't been yet, and anyway preferred her own imaginative pictures from reading the book. He said, 'It's much better if you see the film, because you then get the right pictures – the pictures the author wanted you to have. Otherwise it's not fair on the author.'

Other parents are finding that the less TV and videos they have, the less they encounter child behavioural problems. They recognize that a great deal of TV and computer games are specially designed to wind up their children, so they become more needy and demanding. The result is then even more demands on parents by their children to entertain, to provide stimulation, to buy expensive products and junk food – and for reassurance after disturbing programmes. One of the main effects of advertising on children is that they feel a gnawing sense of dissatisfaction, as if something is missing from their lives.

For myself, living in Gloucestershire, I am grateful for the way in which this special part of England has provided a beautiful environment for the raising of our four children. It has also inspired such writers as J.K. Rowling, Dennis Potter, J.R.R. Tolkien, and Laurie Lee. J.K. Rowling, for example, grew up in the Forest of Dean. She mused that the wild and beautiful Forest (also an inspiration for Fanghorn Forest and the Ents in Lord of the Rings, and Dennis Potter's blue remembered hills of childhood) was an inspiring setting. The lack of things to do – her childhood and teen years spent in relative isolation from any kind of fast-paced media-driven culture – helped to stimulate her imagination. The silence, the walks in the Forest, the practical jokes of the original boy who was the 'model' for Harry Potter, the local legends, the free space for childhood – all of these were crucial for her. Each of these celebrated writers describes their childhood in similar ways – as long, unhurried, with plenty of time to dream, and full of rich experience to treasure for a lifetime.

Their books have been inspirational, providing rich soul-food and meaning. The Harry Potter books, for example, show just how popular a good story is for both children and adults. But with the films, the computer game of 'Find Your Way to the Chamber of Secrets', the junk food, even the Coca-Cola tie-in – Harry Potter has sadly sold out children's minds to commercial interests. I deeply regret and mourn the erosion of childhood under the relentless onslaught of commercialization, rampant materialism, and a fast-paced lifestyle that is demonstrably toxic to children in all kinds of ways. However, as parents we *can* choose to limit media access to our children, and we can also counter the toxic world of the mass electronic media. But such a choice does inevitably mean going against the prevailing commercial and political *Zeitgeist*.

Do you and/or your family suffer from the modern technological disease of *information overload*? Is your family thriving, just surviving, or going under with information fatigue? Do you find when you go on holiday, leaving your electronic media behind, that you're all able to relax?

Consider your daily diet of TV, e-mail, net surfing, news, and advertising. We are exposed to a deluge of information, of hundreds, if not thousands of *advertising messages every day*.[4] At the same time, there is the proliferation of such computer- and TV-related phenomena like stress, eye-strain, sleep difficulties, childhood obesity, 'couch potato' syndrome, repetitive strain injury (RSI), and learning disabilities such as so-called 'Attention Deficit Disorder' (ADD) amongst children. Even Ted Turner of CNN, at the launch of his new Customs News Service, said that 'information smog' had gone too far, dramatically pronouncing that 'It's killing people.'

There is, moreover, a great deal more of the same to come, as information technology becomes ever more sophisticated, prices fall, and access widens. Politicians such as former US President Bill Clinton and British Prime Minister Tony Blair want a computer on every desk for every student in school. Consider the widespread use of hand-held video games, internetted computers, mobile 'phones with video and internet add-ons, and the hundreds of digital TV channels on offer. This is leading to a growing 'screen culture' in children's bedrooms, pushed by technology, by parents' increasing spending on electronic media for their children, and by media-driven fears about 'danger on the streets' – all issues that will be examined later in this book.

Severely numbered are the days when sending children to their bedrooms was considered to be a punishment! Formerly, a television set in the living-room was a central focus of family life, but today, viewing has become 'individualized' into bedrooms, where a burgeoning screen culture now flourishes. In Britain, over a third (36 per cent) of under-fours have a TV set in their bedrooms[5] – and the figure is rising rapidly. Over 70 per cent of children aged 6–17 currently have TVs and videos in their bedrooms, and 36 per cent have computers as well. Some 72 per cent of children have their own bedroom, 68 per cent their own music system, 34 per cent have an electronic games controller hooked up to the TV, and 21 per cent have a video.[6]

According to the 1999 Report *Young People, New Media* – the first full survey for 40 years of the use of the media by children aged 6–17 – children spend over 5 hours per day using the electronic media, including about 2½ hours viewing TV. Most of the children surveyed read books for on average just 15 minutes a day, and perceived books as 'boring, old fashioned, and frustrating'.

Children are also spending less time outdoors, and far more time in their bedrooms, encouraged by parents who are worried about street safety, potential child abuse, and traffic. Only 11 per cent of parents said that the streets where they live were safe for their children. Three children from different parts of London describe vividly why they have opted for the bedroom screen entertainment culture:

'It's like a horror movie outside, it's terrible. I spend almost the whole time in my bedroom watching TV or drawing.'

Ricky Allen, age 10

'Because there's always trouble where I live, I turn on the lights, pull the curtains down, and stay in. When I come back from school, I dump my bag and watch telly.'

Senab Adekunkle, age 15

'I watch lots of TV because there's nothing else to do … I'm not allowed on the road on my bike so I usually stick at home watching TV or something.'

Joanne Mason, age 14[7]

Parents are actually encouraging children to play indoors, therefore, with media-rich bedrooms populated with TV sets, videos, personal computers, and music systems. The extent to which their fears for their children's safety and well-being when playing outside are justified is a big debate, and depends on the local context. However, in spite of well-publicized cases of child abuse and kidnap, figures show that such dangers are no greater than they were 20 years ago. With the advent of traffic-calming measures, road safety has certainly been improving. But perception is everything, and the electronic media themselves tend to overemphasize the likelihood of meeting 'stranger danger', violence, and accidents in public spaces.

The growth of bedroom culture is certainly a cause for concern, with family members living together separately, and children becoming divorced from family culture and shared meal-times. Children exist in media-influenced private worlds that parents may not understand. Television is the main link between the bedroom and the world, but there is now less and less communication about just what is being viewed. Thus, for example, parents and children used to watch more TV together and at least talk about the programmes they had seen. Bedtime is not so much about going to sleep, but about watching some television: according to Sonia Livingstone, one in three children continued watching TV after Britain's 9 p.m. television 'watershed', with 28 per cent of this group aged just 6–8 years.

One clear implication to be drawn from all this is that the electronic media are commonly no longer an integral part of our family environment. Television has usurped and replaced the environment of community life, family, and nature, with many people living inside the virtual reality of the electronic media. Moreover, there exist major struggles for commercial dominance of television and the Internet, as companies increasingly come to realize the ability of these electronic media 'to deliver people's minds'. Liz

King, Microsoft education general manager, made no secret of her commercial intentions when she said, 'Education is a strategic market-place for us. We are educating the next generation of workers who will purchase our products.'[8]

Another implication of these trends is that children are becoming separated from their parents and family culture at ever-earlier ages. Moreover, children are having to adapt to the unhealthy and distorted priorities of modern technological society – for example, where cars take precedence over safe outdoor play spaces. The electronic media offers artificial, imaginary experiences as a replacement for their real experience of nature, and of other people in their families and neighbourhoods. And parents struggling to make a living may both be at work, or so busy with managing the household that TV becomes a convenient electronic baby-sitter that keeps children quiet.

Nor is it just children who are subject to these new cultural forces, for parents are also confronted by the challenge of coping with the electronic media at home and at work. In 1970, 99.5 per cent of homes in North America and Britain had television sets, with at least 95 per cent of people viewing at least some TV every day, and with the average US home keeping the set on for about 8 hours per day. The average adult then watched up to 4½ hours of television per day, and children under 12, 3 hours. Over the last 30 years, TV network viewing figures have slowly declined, a trend that is more marked since the mid-1990s with the rise of video, cable TV, and the Internet. A.C. Nielsen Co. estimated that the average American watches 3 hours and 46 minutes daily, or a full *52 days a year.*[9] By the age of 65, this amounts to nearly *9 years* in front of the tube. Some 40 per cent of households had three or more television sets, with 6 million videos being rented daily.

For families, whereas the average child aged 2–11 watched TV for 1,197 minutes, the time taken by parents in meaningful conversation with their children was only 38.5 minutes – or less than one thirtieth of the time spent watching TV. Put differently, for every minute spent in meaningful conversation, *31 minutes* were spent watching TV. Some 52 per cent of children aged 5–17 had a TV in their bedroom, and 25 per cent of children aged 2–5 had one too. The number of violent acts seen by the age of 18 is 200,000, with 16,000 murders.[10] Yet another deeply disquieting statistic is that an 'average child' may see up to *30,000* commercials in a year, including many junk food ads during one Saturday morning of cartoons.[11]

All in all, a visiting Martian from outer space would surely be very puzzled when observing our worldwide screen culture. Jerry Mander's description of what a Martian might report back to base makes highly sobering reading:

'All the people are watching the same images at the same time. They are even watching in schools. This may be some kind of instrument of mass brain washing or mind control. It seems to be homogenizing values and culture. And the people start behaving like the images they see. This process is going on worldwide. Perhaps we'd best not communicate with this planet. They seem to have lost control of their minds.'[12]

However, there is a growing counter-cultural backlash against intrusive electronic overload and the increasing domination of the electronic media. As we will see later in this book, families are proactively seeking ways to cope with computers and TV so as to reclaim their lives. Whether it is not watching TV at all before children are 7 years of age, or limiting video games, or keeping the computer in the hall-way, many families are beginning to set clear limits to the electronic media. Whilst useful and enjoyable on occasion, computers and TV can also be boring, 'a medium for muggles rather than wizards', as Harry Potter might say! In the USA, *TV*

Free America organizes an annual *TV-Turnoff Week* at the end of April, where families and schools try a life without TV for a week.

As Madonna said of her young child Lourdes, 'TV's poison. To be plopped down in front of a TV instead of being read to, talked to or encouraged to interact with human beings is a huge mistake and that's what happens to a lot of children.'[13]

Notwithstanding all of this disturbing data on modern culture's domination by the electronic media, they are certainly here to stay for the foreseeable future. As parents and educators, we are therefore faced with the challenge of informing ourselves about children's developmental needs, with being committed to developing a culturally rich family life with our children, with developing insight into how the electronic media affect them, and with honing the skills and the will power to control the TV. In sum, then, the main purpose of this book is to identify how to best cope with TV and the computer such that they do not unhealthily dominate and distort family life. The benefit for parents is that this will free up family life for far more enjoyable and satisfying activities. Your golden parenting memories will then be ones of telling your children bedtime stories, or of swimming with them, for example, rather than of watching the TV! ...

So the central questions addressed in this book are as follows:

- What are your observations of your children's TV-watching habits and their use of the electronic media?
- How do happy, healthy, and confident children develop? Do we want hurried, stressed children or children with an authentic childhood?
- What are the effects of TV-watching on children? What is the research evidence on the effects of TV? – so that you can make your own informed decisions about what is right for your child.
- What are the hazards for children of computer use?
- How can families cope successfully with computers and TV?

- How can families furnish a creative, enjoyable, and richly nourishing life together?
- What can schools do to help children and families cope with the electronic media?
- 'It takes a whole village to raise a child': how can communities take up the challenge of coping constructively with the electronic media? And what can we do to counter the increasing pressures of commercialism on childhood?
- What helpful resources and contacts are there?

How to Use This Book

This is a book for dipping into, as and when needed. Some readers will be taking an overview, and considering what is best for themselves and their children – and may want to read the whole book. Others may want to limit media access to their children, and will be looking for research to back up their hunches and intuitions.

Many readers will already have made up their minds about the electronic media in one way or another. They may already be looking for constructive ways of coping, both for themselves and for their partners and children. For such families, Chapters 9 and 10 on constructive ways of coping with TV and computers may well be the most useful.

New parents may want to look ahead, particularly in the light of children's overall development. Some parents will want to use the book to link up with other families, and to develop constructive strategies with their children's schools – which may, of course free up resources previously consumed by information technology for employing another teacher!

Some schools which are concerned with children's overall development – physical, soul, and spiritual – such as schools in the global Steiner (Waldorf) movement, will use this book to underpin their guidelines for the use of the electronic media, as a way of informing discussions and debates about the effects of computers and television in both individual families' lives and in the wider culture. And finally, in the very reading of this book you are actively joining and reinforcing the growing counter-cultural movement of concerned parents and educators who are determined to reclaim a healthy and developmentally nourishing family life from the excesses of the burgeoning 'e-culture' which so affects us all.

2. *'Disturbing Observations'*
Watching Your Child Watching the Television

'What Do You Watch?' ...

When we had a young family, many children visited to play at our home. One 10-year-old girl from up the road just couldn't settle when she first came. She looked everywhere – in cupboards, under the stairs, in the playhouse. It looked like a treasure hunt, and I was mystified until she asked, 'What do you watch?' She found it very strange that there was no TV set anywhere to be found! (In fact, it was hidden away upstairs because we had limited space.)

Claire did have a point, of course – people do just watch. A key and sometimes neglected point is that it is not so much *what* children watch, but *the process of watching itself* that is so important. Thus, TV-watching by itself affects children regardless of programme content – and not least because it displaces other activities such as playing, reading books, and conversation. These wideranging effects can include poor language acquisition, nerves, stress, headaches, bad dreams, eye-strain, hyperactivity, learning difficulties, and poor concentration. Such hazards will be discussed at length in Chapters 4 and 5.

Most parents are usually more concerned about the effects of programme *content*, rather than the amount of time spent watching, or the effects of watching regardless of programme content. Parents are commonly worried about content effects such as violence, poor language, harmful advertising, and the implicit values that programmes propagate, such as 'violent actions by heroes against the baddies are OK'.

So initially, why not try conducting your own experiment by simply observing (as objectively as you can) your child or children watching TV, using computers, and playing computer games. After a few moments you may see that their eyes go vacant and blank, with their mouth slightly open and their body slumped. The hypnotic effects of the television soon take hold. And how is it different with interactive computer games?

Observations of Children Watching Television

A mother described a friend's 2-year-old child watching TV:

> 'He wasn't really watching, he was just sitting there with a glazed expression, as if mesmerized by it. He didn't know what was going on, but only watched because something was moving – the flickering motion attracted him … He was put in front of the box to stop him pestering his mother. He became hyperactive and woke a great deal at night.'

Ellen, who lived in a small flat, thus described her children of 4 and 7 watching television:

> 'They didn't appear to be interested – just looking, just watching the screen, a one-way communication. They had little interest in the programme, but at the same time were glued to it. I noticed it made them quite nervous, and irritable if a

programme was interrupted. If they watch before they go to bed, it makes them restless.'

'Peter would watch TV until it ran out if he was left to himself', his mother observed:

'Children have open minds and are sensitive to all kinds of impressions – for example, the repetitive phrases and the Kung Fu movements Peter picks up. If he watches for a long time, he'll just look like Dumbo for the rest of the evening, with square eyes that are red, quite pig-eyed looking. He'll be aggressive if foiled in what he wants to watch and opposed to what the rest of the family want to do. He seems mesmerized by it constantly coming towards him.'

Time and again, parents describe their children watching TV as 'zombie-like', 'passive', 'stupefied', 'mesmerized', 'totally absorbed but not interested', 'tranquillized', and 'hypnotized'. The exceptions were children watching short programmes with their parents, when there were frequent interruptions by questions and conversations about what was going on. Even then, parents observed how quickly their children lapsed into the 'TV trance-state' of just watching.

Some parents question whether TV-watching was in fact relaxing for their child, noticing that after viewing there often seemed to be signs of edginess, nerves, clumsiness, and outbursts of repressed energy. One mother described her 8-year-old son Adrian's TV habits:

'In winter, he comes home from school, switches on the television to relax, and sits quietly and passively curled up in an armchair. At the end of the children's programmes, he'll jump up, rush out of the door, and tear around the garden on his bicycle.'

Parents commented that viewing seems to 'relax', 'quieten', 'pacify', and 'unwind' their children whilst they were in front of the box. However, afterwards, they are often 'fidgety', 'nervous', 'bolshy', and unco-ordinated – as if waking up from a disturbing dream. This can be characterized as a kind of re-entry process, from the trance-like, TV-viewing state-of-consciousness, and back into waking, day awareness.

After observing their children watching television, many parents are quite shocked by their children's zombie-like 'altered state'. How open and impressionable, yet how passive they appear – in stark contrast to how they are the rest of the time! By comparison, when playing, or reading a book, you can almost *see* their imaginations and minds working, actively and zestfully engaging with the world. If you're telling a story to some 4 or 5 year olds, they are so actively absorbed that they will immediately tell you which detail you missed! One hospital play-therapist told the story of a sick 4-year-old child playing in the ward playgroup. 'When called by his mother to watch *Playschool* on the hospital TV, he shouted back, "No thanks, I'm *in* Playschool!" '

Having observed the effects on their children of TV-watching, or of getting caught up in computer games, some parents are highly disturbed by what they see. If their children are under 7, they often decide either not to allow their children to watch at all, or only to watch a few special programmes together. One father observed what his 5 year old was watching for a few days, and was so upset by what he saw – both programme content and the effects on his child – that they stopped TV-watching altogether. He found the news especially violent and frightening for his child. Young children can certainly be very upset by what they see: for example, many had recurrent nightmares because they just couldn't get over the images of the jumbo jets crashing into the World Trade Centre in New York on 11th September 2001.

A grandmother shared this story of observing her 2-year-old grandson watching television:

> 'The "hero" was driving a car which he then reversed, and it hung precariously with the back wheels almost over the edge of a cliff. There was no panic. The driver said to his wife, "Betty, I don't want to upset you, but sit very still." My little grandson threw himself face downwards on a large cushion, crying out, "No more car! No more car!" Soon after the set was switched off, he kept repeating "No more car". The morning after this occurred, he came to me with a toy car and, balancing it near the edge of the breakfast table, he said, "Look, happen Nanna, happen."'

The grandmother remarked to the boy's parents that she thought TV was not good for him, especially as he had been having disturbed nights. It took a lot of patient conversation to help the boy understand that the TV story was 'just pretending'. Whilst older children can watch terrifying events on TV without reacting, this kind of desensitization may well not be what you want for your child. My now grown-up children still find it amusing that I sometimes cover my eyes and ears at particularly horrific scenes in films!

Box 1

Guidelines for Evaluating Children's TV

1. *News*: The news often has a high violence content, and is designed more and more to be *info-tainment* geared to winning the ratings war. It often offers a highly selective and unrealistic view of the world, and is low on content compared with either radio news or newspapers. Unsuitable

for children up to 11–12 years of age. Try watching with your child to see how they react.

2. *Language*: Try listening to your child's programme with the pictures turned off: is this the kind of language you want your child to learn? – *Uh-Uh! Attem! Argh!* … How do you rate the richness of expression? Is this how you want your children to speak?

3. *Advertising*: One Saturday morning of cartoons had many advertisements for junk food and soft drinks aimed at children. Many programmes, even on BBC or PSB, include product placement advertisements such as football matches. Formula 1 Motor Racing is full of cars and drivers acting like moving billboards. Toy companies produce shows geared to selling their toys and the various add-ons. Even public-service TV such as the BBC may be selling dolls, T-shirts, and accessories at the same time as showing children's programmes like the *Teletubbies*.

4. *Social Skills*: How do people solve problems? – by talking, by discussion, by the strongest 'goodie' winning? Is it all right to take revenge or get your own back, or are alternative ways of solving problems shown? What are the values on offer?

5. *Comprehension level*: Many children are confused by what they see on the screen. It may just be inappropriate for their age – in one study, for example, 4 year olds enjoyed a TV fairy story but were unable to understand it or remember it. They need your help switching off, or discussing what is happening, or in choosing more comprehensible programmes.

6. Watch with your children and ask yourself if you like what you see. Suggest alternative activities to your child, and help them to switch off.

'A Kind of Training for Alienation … ':

One father's discovery on observing his children

Jerry Mander was a successful American advertising professional who realized just how powerful TV is as a medium for placing images in people's heads in order to influence their buying behaviour. He has since written several well-known critiques of television and of technology such as *Four Arguments for the Elimination of Television.* He was also a founder of *Adbusters.*[1]

However, Mander's journey really began when he watched his children playing one day:

'I became alarmed while observing my children watching television, and seeing that blank empty stare on their faces, as the blue light played against them. They seemed like zombies. But an even more frightening realization came to me one day when our whole family was out on a mountainside, picnicking.

My kids were across a meadow playing as I lay on the blanket. I saw them leaping around energetically among the rocks shouting to each other. This looked quite pleasant until I realized that the entire game they were playing was a re-enactment of a television series, *Star Trek.* One child was Captain Kirk, the other Mr Spock, and their lines were right from the TV show. Here we were on this magnificent mountainside, with the sun shining, the flowers blooming, the breezes wafting, but the kids were lost in their TV images. They seemed to be here on the mountainside but their brains were occupied with images of something else. We might as well have been in a subway, or in our living room.

At the time, I didn't realize that this process of implanting imagery that becomes dominant in one's experience was a kind of training for alienation, but I surely do now. But I was uncomfortable at the thought that these implanted images could separate one from nature, and that I had a direct role in it.'[2]

21

So the act of taking time out to observe children watching television, and asking oneself the question, 'How healthy is this activity for my child?' can result in striking and dramatic learning. Many parents have said how this experience was a turning point for them, and how from that moment onwards they trusted their own innate common sense about what was really good for their child.

Another observation exercise is to watch your child with hand-held video games, and using computers, to see the effects for yourself, and to share your observations with your partner or friends. However, there is also the question of how you yourself personally experience the electronic media.

'A Training Ground for Inattention' … : The Zen TV Experiment

Bernard McGrane devised the Zen TV experiment to provoke people into *seeing* television as opposed to just watching it, and to 'stop the world' as the first step in seeing. Try watching TV consciously with mindfulness and precision rather than watching it passively. Ordinarily, if you are watching TV you can't also observe and experience the experience of watching TV. 'When we watch TV we rarely pay attention to the details of the event. In fact we rarely pay attention', writes Bernard McGrane.[3]

Trying the Technical Events Test (TET)

TV programme-makers use technical events such as voice-overs, zooms, changes of music, cuts and superimpositions, and switching views, in order to keep our attention as viewers. 'Pure TV' is like a web camera just recording what's happening, like, for example, closed-circuit television (CCTV) cameras on the high street. Anything different from pure TV is a technical event, part of the craft of making a programme. Forget the programme content, and try just counting the technical events.

When I did the TET with a group of students using a half-minute car commercial, we counted an astounding 130 technical events in that highly crafted short film of just 30 seconds. We watched it over and over again, going through boredom, anger, frustration – 'Why are you doing this head-banging test on us?' – and finally intense interest at the huge resources and technical skill put into honing this half-minute TV gem. No wonder commercials such as this are so successful in grabbing our attention and holding it!

However, you can try these experiments for yourself:

1. Watch any TV show for 10 minutes without turning on the sound, whilst counting the technical events.
2. Watch any news programme for 10 minutes without turning on the sound.
3. Do the same, but just listen without looking at the images at all.
4. Watch the television set for 10 minutes without turning it on!

It is vital for you to try these experiments for yourself, so you can compare your findings with those of Bernard McGrane. He found that:

1. Students get angry and resist the experiment. They asked, 'What is the meaning of this?', saying 'I've wasted 30 minutes of my time'. Eventually, after the fourth exercise, students admitted they had wasted a huge amount of their lives in front of the TV. So why get angry about watching TV without turning it on? …
2. 'When you turn on the TV, you turn the world off.' Why does everything on television appear so real and immediate? Technical events fool us with the *appearance* of being natural and realistic, of being non-produced. But when we do the TET, we are shocked into realizing the extent to which our TV experience

is manufactured. When you focus on the events, you cannot follow the story-line: you either watch the programme *or* count the events. We are presented with short, 'rapid fire' segments of footage. We have to integrate and make sense of these fragments, linking, synthesizing, filling in the blanks and dots.

> 'Our actively synthesizing mind, our labour, goes on while we sit back, relax and absorb. This high-speed integration of often wildly disconnected phenomena (angles, scenes, persons, music) is experienced in the mode of blank and passive absorption. It would seem that our minds are in high gear without our knowing.'[3]

Jerry Mander addresses this observation pointedly:

> 'This difference between internally generated and imposed imagery is at the heart of whether it is accurate to say that television relaxes the mind. Relaxation implies renewal. One runs hard, then rests. When resting, the muscles first experience calm and then, as new oxygen enters them, renewal. When you are watching, your mind ... is certainly not an 'empty mind'. Images are pouring into it. Your mind is not quiet or calm or empty. Maybe nearer to dead, zombie-ized. It is occupied. No renewal can come from this condition.'[4]

3. Jumpy, volatile, scattered, and hyper monkey-minds are induced. The TET shows vividly how TV trains us to reduce our attention spans, how everyday life can be made dull, and how the mind can become jumpy. No wonder some neurophysiologists call television 'a training ground in inattention'. It is a short-term, transient medium, living for the split second, and aiming to glue viewers to the tube, lest ratings decline.

McGrane maintains that:

'It is easier to shorten attention spans and increase distraction rather than to lengthen attention spans, increase concentration, and calm, quieten and still the mind ... The function of TV is to create, maintain and constantly reinforce what – in the Zen tradition – is often called "monkey mind".'[5]

In other words, the tuned-out, scattered, all-over-the-place mind that is out to lunch.

4. The News – subject matter is presented as entertainment. Usually, only highlighted events are shown – the unusual, disasters, wars – rather than everyday events affecting ordinary people ... unless there is an 'entertaining' comic twist to the story. There are much fewer technical events, because the news needs to appear more realistic than other TV shows. Stories are presented as entertainment, and we become greedy for news, as in the CNN or BBC 24 Hours services, which offer the promise of the latest events. Even though TV news presents us with what appear to be 'the facts', in reality this is often an illusion: we just don't know what is happening in Afghanistan; all we receive is a highly selective glimpse and a few edited sound bites. So television becomes a bubble – and the world becomes TV. Seeing is, indeed, believing ...

Night after night in 1999, for example, we were presented with images of NATO bombing Kosovo and Serbia; yet only afterwards did the fact leak out that a mere 17 Serb tanks had actually been destroyed in the exercise.

Box 2

Ways of Keeping Alert while Viewing

Try these screen tests to turn your brain back on when viewing:

1. Count the number of technical events – voice-overs, cuts, zooms; and try spotting how the programme is spliced and edited together.
2. How is the music and soundtrack affecting you?
3. Stretch the scene: widen your view of the screen to take in what's happening off screen – the microphones, set, lights, prompts, etc.
4. Imagine the prompt words above the camera from which the presenter is reading, and which makes him or her so apparently fluent.
5. Measure the status on the news: how much voice and airtime is given to ordinary people?
6. Split the scene: is it the same building when the camera cuts from the outside to an inside scene?
7. TV has to be visual, so count the clichés: e.g. Big Ben used to represent Parliament, or the White House for the US Government.
8. The news given usually favours a particular side – which side?
9. Classify the adverts: the promise, the story, images, thoughts, and feelings. Is the appeal via humour, sex, fun, romance, etc.?
10. Play '*spot the stereotype*': how much diversity of race, gender, age, ability, and class is there?
11. Is there any product placement advertising conveyed in the programme content? Try counting the ads in a football match!
12. What values are guiding the behaviour you see on screen?[6]

What Are Your Own Viewing Experiences?

After doing the TET, try spending some time just observing television, being conscious as you do so of the ways in which your body, your feelings, and your mind respond. Try this exercise even if the programme showing is one you particularly like! Here is an account of one person's experience:

'When I watch, I easily get caught up in the pictures. It is hard to keep my eyes off the screen – they get caught by movements, or attracted by unexpected sounds. The commercials and trailers are much louder than the preceding programme. I feel as though my attention is being compelled, even though I am not particularly interested in the content. Though watching for more than a few minutes makes me restless, I also find it hard to switch off, and may absent-mindedly switch channels, "to see if there is something good on". Afterwards, I feel a bit dulled, need to get up and stretch, get some exercise to feel "together" again. When I watch in the late evening, the TV images tend to live far more vividly than everyday images.'

Many people did remark that they liked viewing because it was relaxing, entertaining, and informative: certainly, for light, discriminating viewers, TV need not be a 'trip'. However, at the same time, they also reflected on the side-effects:

- 'I just can't help watching – it hypnotizes me.'
- ' … the mindless vacancy I get from watching.'
- 'It's like a drug.'
- 'The more I watch, the more apathetic I get, and the less will I have to turn it off.'
- 'Watching drains me of energy.'
- 'I was so vulnerable to TV that I had to get rid of the set altogether.'

Jerry Mander describes his experiences thus:

'My reactions to the experience invariably reduced to one or two constants. Either if the programme I'd been watching had been of some particular interest, the experience felt "anti-life", as though I'd been drained in some way, or I'd been used. I came away feeling a kind of internal deadening, as if my whole body had gone dormant, the victim of a vague soft assault. The more I watched, the worse I'd feel. Afterwards, there was nearly always the desire to go outdoors or to go to sleep, to recover my strength and my feelings. Another thing. After watching television, I'd always be aware of a kind of glowing in my head: the images! They'd remain in there even after the set was off, like an after-taste. Against my will, I'd find them returning to my awareness hours later.'[4]

Tele-addicts and the Plug-in Drug

The commonly observed altered states of consciousness which television induces, the difficulties many people have switching it off, the blank faces, the difficulty remembering programme content – all these disturbing symptoms indicate that television can easily become what Marie Winn graphically called 'the plug-in drug'.[7] Many people describe themselves as 'tele-addicts', spending far more time than they really wish in front of the TV, and feeling unable to control their viewing habits. And whilst you could call television a 'psychological drug', programme makers certainly know how to grab and hold your attention even though you are not particularly interested. Consider the hyper-sophisticated and highly manipulative commercials, with their technical events carefully designed to glue you to the set.

We should also remember that if some adults find it hard to switch off, then children will also find it at least as difficult, and will need adults to help them switch off and make conscious, deliberate decisions about what to watch. And because children's programmes on commercial channels are seen as the means of delivering highly manufactured advertising messages into children's minds – for example, selling toys, computer games, and junk food – then your vulnerable child clearly needs active adult protection from these intrusions.

One of the roots of addiction is the lack of a nourishing environment in the early childhood years. This deeply felt hunger for 'goodness' for the 'something missing' then leads to different forms of addiction later in life. There is a great deal of truth in what Marshall McLuhan said of television, that 'The medium is the massage'.

It is quite natural for young children who are relatively free from the tele-culture to be inherently active, playful, questioning, and engaged in learning about the world. It is therefore *the parents*, and the home environment which they create, that provide the conditions through which children are then susceptible to becoming tele-addicts. For example, TV can so easily be used as 'an electronic baby-sitter', with video and computer games just waiting to be hauled out when televized programmes fail adequately to entertain – or distract …

Parents sometimes fail to follow their own common sense and intuition about what is healthy for their child – or to listen to the wisdom of their own children, as illustrated by the following true story:

'The 4-year-old son of a friend watched a lot of television. His mother sensed that TV was not healthy, but continued to let him watch it. He was subject to nightmares and poor sleep as well as bouts of aggressive behaviour – which was also linked with too much stimulation at home. One night he woke up and screamed that they should throw the TV to the bottom of the garden. Sadly, his parents did not take heed of their young son's desperate, healthy cry. Now, at the age of 6, his mother literally has to engage in a physical fight with him to drag him away from the box.'

Because young children typically need the approval or permission of their parents for their free play and other activities, it is important to be conscious about the ways in which you, as parents, channel your children's activities. Having a snack with your children when they come home from school, and catching up with the day's happenings, is important – not least in enabling them to unwind. However, the underlying effects of TV can lead to feeling *more* wound up, so it's better to play quietly, rest, do some homework, get some exercise, or spend some stress-reducing time with a family pet.

There is a great temptation for parents to encourage their children to watch TV at 'rush hour' times such as before supper. Yet this 'solution' can simply result in a 'vicious viewing cycle' – the more your child watches, the less they play or read by themselves ... and so on, until you as a parent end up feeling that your most important role is to be an entertainer! In sum, the great danger – with quite incalculable lifelong consequences – is that your children end up relying upon *extrinsic* motivation in order to conduct their lives, rather than being encouraged to rely upon *their own* intrinsic creativity, motivation, and imaginative capacities.

In a Nutshell ...

1. Try observing your child watching TV, using computers, and playing video games. How do you feel, and what do you think about what you see?
2. Watch programmes with your child, carefully observing the language used, the images, the pace (use the *Technical Events*

Test), the implicit values, the comprehension level, and the selling (if there is any). Consider how healthy this experience is for your child?

3. Do the *Zen TV experiment* on yourself – how do you experience TV-watching? Are you in control or not?

4. TV can routinely be used by parents as a plug-in drug. One viable alternative is to guide your children toward making their own activity choices in a way that avoids the dangers of tele-addiction.

5. Children naturally imitate their parents – so if you watch a lot of TV, so will they!

6. The electronic media are extremely powerful, geared to keeping your attention even if you're not especially interested – so young children need you to switch off the television, and older children also need help with developing *their capacity to choose* to switch off.

3. *The Secrets of Child Development*

'But the TV has spent so much more time raising us than you have.'

Lisa to Homer in *The Simpsons*

There is nothing like a wise grandparent! When staying with their daughter a few months after the birth of her first child, the visiting grandparents found the baby to be nervy and prone to excessive crying, with sleeping difficulties. The cause seemed to be the television, which was switched on near the baby for a lot of the time. So the grandfather tactfully mentioned that the TV might be a cause, suggesting the father ask his mother-in-law about the effects of the TV on babies. 'After all, just as you are an expert in finance, so your mother-in-law as a teacher has lifelong expertise in what helps and hinders child development.' So the grandmother suggested no TV at all for a week to see what the effects would be on the baby. The child soon calmed down and began to sleep well, and as a result, the TV was seldom put on whilst the children were young.

However, it is not only some parents who lack the knowledge of how healthy children develop; it can be some teachers too. A 7-year-old boy entered a Californian state school. He was not getting on well and was clearly anxious, experiencing nervous twitches and nightmares. His mother went to discuss his problems with his teacher. 'Well you see', said his teacher, 'your son is not watching enough TV and videos. He doesn't play computer games such as Nintendo, which speeds up reactions.' The teacher recommended a Disney Game Boy, and Pokemon videos. The mother was appalled, and asked, 'But surely it is better for him to learn to play creatively and use his own imagination?' 'Well. Yes, I agree with you', replied the teacher. 'But it has been shown that the skills developed by these games actually enable boys to become good fighter pilots!'

So his mother sent her son to a Steiner (Waldorf) school where children's use of the electronic media is carefully limited. 'We again have a thriving, blossoming, vital, energetic, enthusiastic, full-of-life 8-year-old boy who no longer has a nervous twitch, who now sleeps well, and is free of headaches.'[1]

Parents can benefit from access to practical knowledge about what helps healthy child growth and development, so as both to back up their own good sense, and also to cope with the relentlessly increasing pressures in modern culture. Such pressures include the withering-away of the extended family – with relatives and grand-parents typically no longer living nearby. Gone, then, are our tradi-tional support networks; and a smaller family means that you no longer learn childcare at your parents' or neighbours' knees. Changing work patterns are also forcing parents to juggle between children and work. However, more sound, reliable information than ever before is now available about positive ways of raising chil-dren, as paradoxically there is more pressure than ever for children to grow up too fast, too soon.

Too Much Too Soon, or the Right Thing at the Right Time?

The raising of children is one of life's toughest, most satisfying, and rewarding challenges. However, many parents may lack the requi-site skills and knowledge needed to support confident childcare.

Somehow, books and childcare experts aren't enough, so we look to other parents for help. Antenatal groups and parenting courses often develop into support networks, as the other parents you meet become friends. This process of finding support continues when your child starts in a parent and toddler group, Kindergarten, playgroup, or school proper. The parents of your children's friends often become your friends as well.

New parents can often feel isolated from the community, however, having hitherto focused on study or work. Some may take time to understand just how happy, healthy children develop. However, it is useful to grasp the precise nature of children's developmental needs. Julia Childs, the well-known American cook, says that 'Good cooks need principles, not recipes.' So if you do possess insight into your children's developmental needs, you'll be far more likely to know what is healthy for your child without recourse to 'experts' or self-help manuals.

It's hardly surprising, then, that many children are suffering from stress: they feel hurried, fobbed off by their parents' notions of 'quality time'; and they are encouraged to do too many things and feel too busy. As a consequence, children can then withdraw early to their bedrooms after school, putting on pyjamas as a defensive sign that they have simply had enough! The Yale University child psychologist Professor David Elkind first noticed this tendency to hurry children, who were manifestly growing up too fast, too soon. He observed that:

'Hurried children are forced to take on the physical, psychological, and social trappings of adulthood before they are prepared to deal with them. We dress our children in miniature adult costumes, often with designer labels, we expose them to gratuitous sex and violence, and we expect them to cope with an increasingly bewildering social environment – divorce, single parenthood, and homosexuality. Through all these pressures, the child senses that it is important for him or her to cope without admitting the confusion and pain that accompanies such changes. Like adults, they are made to feel they must be survivors, and surviving means adjusting – even if the survivor is only six or eight years old.'[2]

The aim of this chapter, therefore, is to provide a succinct 'map' of the natural path of healthy growth and development which children tread from birth, as a baby, toddler, infant, child, and then adolescent, through to being a young adult. This guide will, in turn, help you to decide just what is appropriate for your child for facilitating rather than interfering with and impeding this developmental process; and it will provide you with an indispensable backdrop against which you, as parents and educators, will be able to make more informed media-related choices.

Children Take Their Time

Just as 'hurry' is the enemy of love, so 'hurry' also gets in the way of raising happy, secure, and healthy children. Children take their time to grow. The unhurried pace of child growth is important for enabling the brain and nervous system to develop fully by the early twenties. Children are not machines or bio-computers: their emotional, physical, cognitive, and personal development form an integrated whole. Feeding the child's body, soul, and spirit, and offering a balance of secure limits and freedom for learning, together facilitate healthy growth.

Phases of child development: babies and toddlers

Children grow through a series of life phases. These are like a sequence of unfolding births that the child undergoes – births that are accompanied by a process of becoming more physically and psychologically independent. Each 'birth' initiates the development of the new physical and psychological possibilities that characterize the emerging phases.

The most obvious birth is the physical birth from the mother, although the baby will take a few years to become emotionally independent from her. For the first few years of life, the baby, toddler, and infant is tenderly open to the environment – as Rudolf Steiner put it, as if he or she were like a 'total sense organ' which is influenced by every happening.

In his book *Birth without Violence*, Dr Leboyer describes how sensitive the newborn baby is to noise, bright lights, rough movements, and rough handling with cold or warm hands.[3] He maintains that through providing a gentle environment for the birth, similar to the dark, warm, gravity-free womb with its constant reassurance of the maternal heartbeat – and which the baby is leaving and losing – the entry into the physical world is eased. Babies and young children, then, are all 'sense organs' – like a sack of flour, *their very being* registers every impression made upon them. The newborn baby is open, sensitive, and vulnerable – an unfinished creature who is now dependent on the care of her parents and on the quality of her home environment.

The only defence a baby possesses against troublesome sense impressions is to sleep or to cry – or, possibly, to cut off mentally, with physical escape being impossible. Their task is to learn to filter and organize sense impressions – for example, they take up to 1–2 months to smile or cry in response to parental attention. The baby's body becomes her toy to be explored, chewed, sucked, and felt – along with other objects and people. With the ability to sit up, she can handle things and focus on objects at some distance. It is a joy to observe a baby quivering with the enjoyment of being nursed, or grasping a beloved object, or seeing and recognizing a parent.

With crawling and standing up, the vertical dimension is explored – as also happens when the baby drops things from her high chair for others to pick up. Eventually she begins to walk with enjoyment and concentration.

During these first years, the acquiring of motor skills – to hold up the head, to sit up unsupported, to manipulate the arms, hands, and legs, to roll over, to crawl, to feed, and to stand – results in the patterning of the growing brain and the development of the central nervous system's responses.[4] These motor skills need to be exercised when the baby wishes. Parents who hold, cuddle, play with, and stimulate their baby are assisting in its development. Babies that are left alone too much or are over-stimulated – or left near the television – may well suffer as a consequence.

The toddler

When the baby first walks and becomes a toddler, a necessary condition for well-being is that of trust in the goodness and support of her parents. The toddler is an experimenter in movement – climbing, rolling, running (before walking), lurching haphazardly into things, practising jumps, leaning, and toppling over.

The toddler learns through the power of imitation – she instinctively imitates the adults and children around her. To see my then 2-year-old son and 6-year-old daughter imitating my wife and myself so faithfully could certainly make for hilarious entertainment! They caught our exact gestures, intonations, favourite family expressions, and mannerisms. This illustrates how young children soak up experiences like blotting paper – they absorb all the habits, feelings, tensions, joys, sorrows, and behaviour of the adults they imitate. Children with violent parents will tend to copy violence; those with loving parents will tend to imitate that behaviour. As psychologist Steve Biddulph says, the number one rule of child psychology is that the children are *not* the problem; it's far more often the parents – or the culture …

Toddlers are great explorers of their surroundings, with their fingers and tongues busy opening cupboards, tipping out the contents, feeling different textures, messing about with sand and water, experimenting with things. They need to experience at first hand the reality and 'goodness' of the world – to touch, taste, smell, hear, see, and feel their world.

The first three years of life see the growing child learning to walk, to speak, and to think. It has been said that a child learns more in the first three years than in the whole of the rest of its life.

The development of language and speech emerges from the primeval 'babble' of babies and the mutual language of love, closeness, and signs between parents and child. A real person wanting to communicate with a baby is the precondition for language development. Young children can only learn to speak properly through real contact with real speaking human beings; and it cannot be too strongly emphasized that *no technological stand-in, no matter how sophisticated, can ever substitute for such real human contact.*

From babble, signs, and gesture emerges the ability of a baby to imitate a specific sound, and then the utterance of some syllables at around 9 months to a year old. The inner world of what the toddler hears and understands, which will become the basis of thinking, is continually enriched by the surrounding people having real conversations both with her and with each other.

In the second year, toddlers may start 'naming' things – like Adam walking around in the Garden of Eden – and gaining great delight from this process. Words are played with, simply from the joy of sound and the delight of muscular activity of the tongue that's required. Our own children enjoyed deliberately using sound words like 'basgetti' for spaghetti, for example.

When, in about the third year, a child begins to say 'I' to herself – 'I want' instead of 'Want' or 'Pauline want' – she has named herself as the centre of her experiences, feelings, and behaviour. The child's inner language and speech continue to develop so that words are increasingly used to communicate feelings, replacing the old sign language. The full development of speech and language may normally take up to the age of 6 or 7 and beyond.

The first three years, then, are absolutely crucial to a person throughout life. Sensory, emotional, and physical deprivation will retard children, whilst over-stimulation will make them nervy, discontented, and restless. The child's sense impressions will be built right into their sensitive organisms, since unlike adults they find it far more difficult to filter or screen out unwanted information. All in all, the home environment has far-reaching effects. If parents choose to put their baby to sleep in front of the television, or choose to leave their 2 year old to the mercy of fast-paced electronic imagery on television when their delicate senses are so vulnerable, this will most certainly have deep-rooted effects.

The infant: 3–6 years – a time to play

Each phase of childhood needs to unfold in an all-round way in order that the foundation for the next phase can be fully prepared; and the present account therefore offers a general map rather than one that fits every child. Each child develops at his or her own pace – although walking, speaking, thinking, and the ability to say 'I' are usually accomplished by around the third birthday.

The infant gradually acquires her physical independence, mobility, and co-ordination in the world. She can dress herself, tie shoelaces, wash, sleep all night without being wet – by the age of 5 or 6. All kinds of play activities are engaged in: indeed, it's sometimes said that 'an infant's work is its play'. What adults are doing – such as cleaning the house, washing up, gardening, digging, driving, cooking, childcare, and baking – is imitated in play. Imitation gives way to the magic of playing. A sheepskin rug is transformed into a boat; a green sheet becomes its sail, the chair a mast, and the carpet the sea. A piece of Plasticine turns into a hearing-aid for dolly, a straw becomes a stethoscope with which to play *Doctors*. Bits and pieces, old clothes, old dolls are juggled with in all kinds of imaginative ways.

Dolls which are too detailed and life-like, or exact copies of objects, tend to stultify the imaginative magic that can be wrought by infants on a few pieces of cloth. This playing is hard work – as any adult who has tried to play along with them for any length of time will acknowledge!

Infancy also needs the nourishment of songs, rhymes, and stories that lead children practically and imaginatively into a deeper relationship with the earth, stones, plants, trees, animals, and the people around them. The time-honoured nursery rhymes, games, songs, and stories seem to have been custom-built for infants to acquire a wide vocabulary, a sense of rhythm, a sense for numbers, a feel for language, and a deepened imagination.

Conversations with adults are important. It is necessary to answer children's questions carefully but not with pedantic, over-rational information. The incessant 'Why … ?' stage and the repetitive question, which can be so irritating to a busy or preoccupied adult, are not so much an asking for information but, rather, represent the need for the reassurance which repetition provides. Then come the 'why, where, when, how, and what' questions stemming from a bubbling interest in people and in life. In a busy day there may not be much time for such brief conversations – although meal-times often afford a good opportunity. I always found our young children needed to talk before going to sleep, to look over the day, and to discuss troublesome or special things.

Physically the infant becomes more independent of her parents, and begins to meet the world directly, on its own terms. Movement in space is conquered as motor skills are refined, manual dexterity emerges with such activities as painting or block building, balance is acquired, and the left/right orientation is gradually learnt.

Socially, new habits are acquired as the infant becomes more self-aware – conscious of herself and her place amongst friends in the home or in the playgroup. She has to get on with others, to play together with other children, to become used to a little brother or sister, to relate to mother and father in new ways.

A sense of time also has to be cultivated. From birth onwards, the baby has to learn to sleep and wake, which is the first activity of rhythmic time-sequencing. Personal adult memory generally only goes back to the period when, as a child, one can first say 'I' for oneself.

Only in later years can you call up early memories at will. Each day is a complete unity in itself for the child, and her sense of identity is fostered when the same sequence of events takes place regularly, as time for children is as vast as space. Most of us can recall how long it was from one birthday to the next, from Christmas to Christmas. It is the rhythm of regular habits, the progression of one season to the next, which gradually establishes the dawning sense of self within the changing pattern of life.

The heart of childhood: 6–12 years

Having mastered her physical body and 'played' her way into the world, the infant undergoes a 'life crisis' in the sixth or seventh year. This is marked by the loss of the milk teeth and the second dentition. During the child's first seven years her energies have been largely involved in forming, organizing, and mastering her physical body.

By 6 or 7, the physical organization and neuromuscular functions are complete, which releases the body-structuring biological forces for other purposes. These liberated forces are taken up into the child's life of picture thinking and of imagination. At this stage, the child can begin to separate an object, which she sees from the inner picture or idea she has of it. She can separate her imagination from the things she is playing with: for example, she can begin to represent more characteristically in her drawing the house or person she has in mind. This liberation of forces hitherto devoted to physical growth and development can be described as another 'birth' ... the birth of a more independent imagination and a capacity to place thoughts in a sequence that is more understandable to the logically thinking adult. Interestingly enough, this comes just after the brain's maximum rate of growth for the early years has been reached, for this begins to slow down from 5 or 6 years of age.

Traditionally, the time for school proper, for learning to read, to write, and work with numbers was in the seventh year.[5] Just as children need space and time to learn to walk, to speak, and to play before extra demands are made upon them, so children's *intellectual* and *cognitive* development should not be forced prematurely before their growth forces (which are becoming available for thinking and imagination) are fully free from their vital 'building work' in the physical body. Learning to read and to write too early, therefore, may leave subtle weaknesses in the growing bodies of children.

Development then unfolds through the 'heart of childhood' phase, from 7 to approximately 11 years of age. Heightened creative possibilities abound in this period, as children's imaginative capacities come to the fore. Children grow out of the 'learning through imitation and play' phase, toward creating together in artistic and many different ways. The imaginative life is vivid, and there is a thirst for stories. Thus, fairy tales, fables, myths, and legends are a source of rich nourishment for children's developing inner life. At this stage, children love pictures, and making their own pictures.

Children's creative capacities should be encouraged in all kinds of ways, for example through play-acting, story-telling, painting, music, crafts, modelling, and games. It is partly through games that children learn about social life, about how to make, break, and change the rules of different games, and about how to prepare for the great 'game' of social life.

Language develops beyond a 'toy', as Jean Piaget describes its use in the early years, and as a medium for giving commands in the process of playing. It becomes a social means of communication about feelings, likes, and dislikes. A feeling for poetry, rhyme, and meaning, often entrenched in the age-old jingles of 'children's culture', emerges.

The birth of likes and dislikes – of the emotional world – encourages children to explore such opposites as good-bad, beautiful-ugly, rich and poor in their feelings. Through stories, plays, or games, children learn to clarify their own shades of feeling and personal values within the inner realm of feeling that is opening up. Just as once the world of space and time was explored in infancy, so now the world of feeling is being carefully charted.

A consequence of this imaginative exploration of feeling is a dawning sense of inner conscience, of morality, of what is right. Infants cannot understand why an action is wrong, although a 4 year old will agree to what a loved grown-up says is right or wrong. For such a child, breaking three plates accidentally may be 'more wrong' than breaking one deliberately! Later, at 6 or 7, children may still accept adult judgements about right or wrong actions – but they will be helped, for example, by imaginative stories about how the friend felt from whom they stole a beloved toy. Instead of dogmatic moral statements, children need to experience *in their feelings* the hurt, loss, or tears caused in others by their actions. This prepares the way for being able to feel personally responsible for one's actions, to be able to reason about right and wrong, and to the acquiring of standards or ground rules to guide behaviour.

The so-called 'ninth-year crisis' recognized by Steiner (Waldorf) pedagogy shows itself in such events as children wondering if parents are really theirs, in testing out the teacher's authority, and in feelings of doubt and of aloneness. The world of imagination and of outer reality split apart – there is no longer a magic formula for imaginatively transforming the world. The child experiences herself on an island – as a more independent self – an experience prefacing the development of a mature adult individuality much later on. Children need help in achieving a more conscious relationship between the factual world and their inner world – through a loving but realistic study of animals or plants, for example. Trust and confidence need to be re-established with teachers and parents on a new level, one that recognizes that these adults are perhaps not all-knowing after all.

Successfully encountered, the ninth-year crisis brings to a child a greater awareness of past, present, and future – of the consequences of actions. The moral sense of conscience begins to develop. Time takes on a new dimension, and she can relate happenings from the past and connect them with the future. 'When I was little … ' comes into the conversational vocabulary; and 'When I'm twelve … ' – a milestone of huge dimensions of freedom – 'I'll be able to do … '.

Moral perception, the sense of conscience, begins to appear, and this needs to be fostered by stories, by biographies, and through history – for example, the problems Moses had in guiding the Children of Israel to the promised land; the troubles of the Norse Gods with Loki, never quite knowing whether he was helping or hindering their purposes. Such stories as the time-honoured account of King Alfred and the cakes highlights dramatically the problems of justice and objectivity in social encounters. The social awareness of the growing child can be prepared from stories and imaginative pictures so as to feed the critical faculties of the growing intellect that heralds approaching puberty.

Eva Frommer summarizes the years from 7 to 10 as follows:

'So during these four years, the child traverses immense fields of experience that are open to him only at this time, and at no other, in quite such a natural way. They teach him about feelings and ill feelings; they teach him about the living world as part of himself, of his own experience; they teach him about his fellows. And in him there grows the need to become a fellow-man and live, learn and work together as well as commune with his kind. Lastly, at the end of this period, he comes rather abruptly to a meeting with himself, standing between his inner and his outer life, and seeking a bridge. This is indeed an epic journey and requires the right understanding, guidance and companionship from the adults who are responsible for his care.[16]

At 11 and 12, children are on the threshold of a new phase of experience – that of puberty and of adolescence. Unless puberty has already been encountered, there can be a unique grace and poise with children of this age. The great creative talents and verve of the 'heart of childhood' period continue to thrive, whilst the ability to think more logically and objectively may be developing strongly. Traditionally, the twelfth year was the time when children made a transition to the more intellectually oriented secondary school, a change that coincided with the stronger emergence of the logical faculties.

By the age of 12 or so, the senses and the brain have matured to the point where the left and right hemispheres are more specialized, and the connecting bridge of the corpus callosum is fully developed. However, this maturing process continues more slowly through the teenage years. Brain imaging research indicates that teenagers' brains are still maturing, and that the biological changes that enable feelings to be well integrated with thinking and judgement may not occur until the early twenties.

Individual Differences between Children's Relationships to the Screen

Insight into general childhood development is, of course, helpful, but understanding your individual child – how they react to situations and people – is also useful. In his book *Children are from Heaven*, John Gray describes the four temperaments of young children: the active or choleric child, the sanguine or responsive child, the sensitive or melancholic child, and the receptive or phlegmatic child.[7]

Active children: sometimes referred to as 'choleric', they like doing things, getting results, and are energetic. They may soon tire of TV as the experience is too passive for them – unless it's an all-action programme. They don't feel comfortable with sitting around, and computer games requiring action may be more interesting. They need structure – a parent who gives direction and clear rules so they know where they are and can feel secure. Think of Tigger in *Winnie the Pooh*!

Sensitive children: known also as 'melancholic', they are more inward, vulnerable, and full of feeling – with an acute awareness of how they respond to others. They appreciate being listened to and being understood by their parents, and they need a lot of empathy. They bear the suffering of the world – and need to know that you suffer too. They can become isolated – and leaving them to the TV by themselves can reinforce their isolation, as well as the programme content sometimes overloading their sensitivity. They can withdraw and get deeply troubled by what they see – unlike the active, choleric child who can shrug it off more easily. Eeyore is a melancholic!

Responsive children: these 'sanguine' children like change, stimulation, have many interests, and are social and outgoing. They live in the moment, and come alive in a vivid sensual experience of the world. They can flit like butterflies from one thing to another – often leaving things in chaos or half-finished. They are easily distracted, and may soon forget what you asked them to do or what they were doing. They enjoy reacting to life's experience and need stimulation, but can throw tantrums if they don't want to move on. If left to the screen, they can be caught by the ever-changing images – and this can really over-stimulate them. They especially need help in switching off – as they may like the TV on just to watch the flashy bits. And computer games, of course are highly designed to hold attention, so they will also need your help in using these with sparing discrimination. But it is also easy to distract them with another activity that's more interesting, so that you can then quietly switch off the set! Piglet is an example of a sanguine or responsive type. And finally,

Receptive children: these so-called 'phlegmatic' types need a regular daily rhythm, like Winnie the Pooh with his snacks at elevenses and at four o'clock. They don't like surprises, and want to know what to expect – they like routine, repetition, rhythm, and order, from which they derive a sense of comfort. They enjoy time passing, like day-dreaming, just sitting and watching – and economies on effort. So when an active sister has tried balancing bricks over and over again, a receptive child, having observed carefully, may balance the bricks right first time! But if left alone with television, or with computer games, they may get into an ingrained habit that gives them comfort and is difficult to change. So they need parents' help by giving them tasks, or through helping them to develop their own interests. They also need rituals, like a bed-time story every night, a boiled egg and toast every Sunday breakfast, and swimming twice a week!

Although this framework of the temperaments is a useful guide, it is also important to remember that *every child is a unique individual*; and though it is common for one of the temperaments to predominate in childhood, over the years these become more balanced. However, John Gray's strategies for communicating really do work:

- listening and understanding with the sensitive child;
- structure and rules with the active child;
- distraction and re-direction for responsive children; and
- ritual and rhythm for receptive children.

These are very useful tips if you want to limit screen use and to substitute healthy alternatives instead.

In a Nutshell ...

1. Children take time to develop, and need raising in a secure, loving, nourishing home. They need a balance of the freedom to learn, safe boundaries, and good food and nourishment for the body, soul, and spirit.
2. Given the complex, step-by-step path of child growth and development, how can we help children to enjoy what is appropriate at the right time, as opposed to hurrying them into 'too much too soon'?
3. The electronic media over-stimulate babies, toddlers, and young children, who are essentially vulnerable and open to the world.
4. Children thrive when they are loved, where their developmental needs are respected, and when they are allowed to have an authentic childhood.
5. Young children learn first-hand about the real world through their whole bodies and senses, through movement and play. They are not 'couch potatoes' by nature! Parents can consciously choose to hold back the electronic media and the virtual world for later, when older children and teenagers possess more resources for coping, and a more developed capacity for mature, conscious discernment.

How, then, do the electronic media affect children and their growth?

4. *Physical Hazards of Screen Culture I*

Effects on the Brain and the Senses

'I thought that television would be the last great technology that people would go into with their eyes closed. Now you have the computer.'

Neil Postman[1]

Such is the range of physical and physiological hazards to children resulting from screen culture that their thorough consideration requires two full chapters. In this chapter, the effects of screen culture upon the brain and the senses will be examined, and in Chapter 5 I look in detail at the questions of light, and of the various movement injuries (i.e. repetitive strain and musculo-skeletal injuries).

Parents often ask, 'What is the right age for my child to start watching TV or use a computer?' This is a key question; and it is important that each and every family take the responsibility to make up its own mind, calculating their own overall 'balance-sheet' of the advantages and the hazards of the electronic media for their children – an assessment which reading this book will help families to reach. The purpose of this and the following chapter, then, is to provide a wide-ranging overview of the research evidence on screen culture's pervasive physical, social and emotional/behavioural side-effects. Families can then use this information to make appropriate decisions and choices from a more informed standpoint.

Box 3

The story of the introduction of new electronic media technologies has not been guided by the precautionary principle of first researching their side-effects. In the 1950s, for example, many TV owners got more radiation from their sets than they did from the fall-out from nuclear tests![2] A recent example is how researchers found that young children absorb up to 50 per cent more radiation in their brains when they use mobile phones. Radiation penetrates half-way through the brain of a 5 year old because their skulls are smaller and thinner. Although researchers think that the evidence for mobile phone radiation posing a health risk is inconclusive (not least because long-term longitudinal research has not yet been possible), concerns have been raised about the potential link with brain tumours, memory loss, irregular brain activity, and headaches. Following a report by Sir William Stewart, the British government has given a health warning that mobile users under 16 should limit calls for essential purposes and keep calls as short as possible.[3]

There is much research on the hazards of the electronic media for children. Since TV and computers both use the cathode-ray tube (CRT, or VDT) (although the kinder liquid crystal screens are now spreading), they will be grouped together under the term 'the electronic media'. The Alliance for Childhood's important research report *Fool's Gold* sets out a useful typology of screen culture's health effects, the framework of which is summarized in Box 4.

Box 4

Potential Health Hazards of the Electronic Media

Too much exposure to the electronic media may risk the following potential health hazards and developmental blocks in young children:

Physical effects

- Difficulty switching off
- Blunted senses, visual strain, and under-stimulation of the developing brain
- Health and light
- Side-effects of toxic emissions and electromagnetic radiation Repetitive strain injury (RSI) – musculo-skeletal injuries
- Childhood obesity, lack of exercise, and movement disorders

Social and emotional effects

- Social isolation and withdrawal
- The plug-in drug: electronic addiction
- Undermining of play
- Commercial exploitation
- Anti-social behaviour

Cognitive effects

- Disorganized brains
- Less creativity and imagination
- Undermining of language and literacy
- Attention deficit and inability to concentrate
- Lean and mean view of the world
- Educational effects

Moral effects

- Exposure to inappropriate material such as violence, and pornography
- Desensitisation from information overload.[4]

The Wide Range of Physical Effects

Why is it hard to switch off?

The electronic media are easy to switch on but hard to switch off. The causes of this difficulty lie both in the content as well as the medium. Either way, children need help switching off because the TV/VDT inhibits the brain functions that are involved in the decision-making process.

How are eyes glued to the tube?

Electronic scanning generates television or computer 'images'. Countless small phosphor dots, formed into 625 lines (or 525 in North America) are activated by a cathode ray gun scanner, which fires electrons along alternate lines. In one thirtieth of a second, the scanner sweeps twice across the screen to activate the alternate lines of phosphors. The eye receives each dot, and this is transmitted to the brain. The brain then 'fills in' the dots of each scanner pattern, below the level of our conscious awareness. The only image is the one we create in our brain – by linking up the required dots – a scatter of dots like a tea strainer or like a children's colouring book where lines have to be connected between dots.

The generation of illumined dots at 30 (or 50) times per second puts a strain on the visual system, since the eye and the conscious brain can only record visual stimuli at 20 impulses or less per second. The experience of 'not quite keeping up' with the electronic pace of the scanner is one physical factor implicated in the 'gluing' of eyes to the tube.

You may have had the common experience of being in a room with a TV set on. Even though the programme content is of no interest to you, and one is doing something else, one's eyes often wander and 'get caught' by the screen.

'Viewing is at the conscious level of somnambulism'

Australian researchers Fred and Merrelyn Emery have suggested a second cause of the inability to switch off. They believe that the special kind of light that CRTs give off 'closes down' the mind. The human nervous system finds it hard to cope with the light because, firstly, it is 'radiant' and not 'ambient' light, and secondly because it is rapidly switching on and off.

Most objects we look at leave our eyes alone – they give off ambient, or reflected light. But if you look at a light source itself, you get radiant light at a high intensity. The Emerys argue that the human perceptual system has evolved to deal with ambient light, *not* radiant light. As the evolutionary process has not developed human sight for looking at radiant light, we don't try to do it: we just cut off.

The second cause of the mind closing down is the rapidly pulsating light – on and off, 50 or 60 times per second. This rapid pulsation produces 'habituation' – i.e. the brain gets used to the rate of light pulses, and becomes fixated by them, so that the content of the programme is displaced. The Emerys likened the television to a technological hypnotist, with the brain dominated by the signal: 'Provided the viewers continue to watch, they are unlikely to reflect on what they are viewing.'

The hypothesis that television functions as a radiant repetitive light source that closes down the brain may explain why many people describe themselves as 'mesmerized' or 'hypnotized' by the medium. Observe people viewing – the 'television stare', the fixed position of the eyes and head, the minimal movement of the eyes, which take in the whole screen in a slightly de-focused way. In normal vision, by contrast, the eyes are continually moving and focusing. As focused eyes are usually a sign of conscious attention, then the 'Zombie-look' of viewers may be understood as indicating a trance-like, semi-conscious, or dreaming state of consciousness. The Emerys believed that 'Viewing is at the conscious level of somnambulism.' In other words, viewers are held barely awake by the medium.[5]

The Emerys based their findings on experiments which have comprehensively shaken up the way in which television is used for product and political advertising. The way in which the 'TV/Brain phenomenon' could give 'direct access to peoples' minds' was, in fact, discovered by accident.[6]

The TV/Brain phenomenon

The TV/Brain phenomenon has been researched since the 1980s, because advertisers realized that the electronic media possessed the great advantage of giving them direct access to people's minds. Tony Schwartz, former US President Jimmy Carter's media advisor, said that 'We are not concerned with getting things across to people so much as getting things out of people. Electronic media are particularly effective tools in this regard because they provide us with direct access to people's minds.'[7]

Whilst the television may be switched on for long periods, people may only be watching intermittently. This is ideal for advertisers or those seeking attitude changes via television. Tony Schwartz, who used TV 'as a door to your home, even as a door to your mind', wrote that: 'Recent attitude change has shown that the most favourable condition for affecting someone's attitude involves a source the listener depends on or believes in, and yet one he does not actively or critically attend to.'[8]

Herbert Krugman, later to become manager of public opinion research at General Electric Connecticut, researched into the physiological responses of the brain to television-watching. Using electrodes attached to subjects' heads, he observed brainwave patterns on an electroencephalograph. With repeated trials with TV viewers, within 30 seconds the brainwaves switched from beta waves – indicating alert and conscious attention – to alpha waves. The latter indicate an unfocused, receptive lack of attention – a condition of subconscious day-dreaming and aimless wandering. Krugman was impressed at how quickly the alpha state emerged. For readers of books and magazines, beta waves appeared – a sign of alertness, attention, and waking consciousness.

Another experiment had ten children watching their favourite TV programme. Dr Eric Pepper of San Francisco State University hypothesized beforehand that because the children were interested, brainwave patterns would alternate between beta and alpha waves. However, 'They didn't do that. They just sat back. They stayed almost all the time in alpha. This means that while they were watching they were not reacting, not orienting, not focusing, just spaced out.'[9]

One explanation of the TV/Brain phenomenon is that television closes down the logical left brain, leaving the right hemisphere open to incoming images. The left hemisphere of the brain is concerned with sequential logic, words, analysis, and reasoning. It processes only one stimulus at a time, leading to orderly sequences of thought. The left brain 'tunes out' when viewing TV. The right hemisphere is concerned with images, colours, rhythms, and emotions – processing information emotionally and non-critically. The left brain takes in the *content* of what someone says, the right brain takes in the non-verbal gesture, tone of voice, and gaze.

Whilst viewing, the non-critical right brain can work unhindered. Krugman wrote in his report:

'It appears that the mode of response to television is more or less constant and very different from the response to print. That is, the basic electrical response is clearly due to the medium and not to content difference. Television is ... a communication medium that effortlessly transmits huge quantities of information not thought about at the time of exposure.'[10]

The Emerys also considered that viewing decreases vigilance and preparedness for action:

'The nature of the processes carried out in the left cortex and particularly area thirty-nine (the common integrative centre) are those unique to human as opposed to other mammalian life. It is the centre of logic, logical human communication and analysis, integration of sensory components and memory, the basis of man's conscious, purposeful and time-free abilities and actions. It is the critical function of man that makes him distinctively human.'[11]

To conclude, the TV/Brain phenomenon may well account for why it is hard to switch off the electronic media. The medium tunes out the logical left brain, and tunes in the uncritical right cortex, which processes images 'not thought about at the time of exposure'. Not only is it hard to switch the set off, but also the medium puts one into a semi-conscious/half-dreaming state – 'spaced-out'.

Resisting 'the basic electrical response of the brain to the medium'

However, according to the findings of brain hemisphere research, it is possible to choose the mode of thinking with which we embrace an activity. Certainly, for many uses of the computer such as word processing, spreadsheets, e-mail, and games, we need to be alert.

However, according to researchers such as Krugman and the Emerys, we need to expend extra effort on such tasks because our minds are *resisting* 'the basic electrical response of the brain'. This could explain some of the fatigue we experience when working with computers.

Robert Ornstein, a leading brain researcher, suggests that the left and right brains are specialized for the kind of thinking people choose to use. This type of thinking need not be controlled by the medium they confront. TV viewers can therefore watch analytically and critically – noting camera angles, editing sound-image links, frames. However, if one does this (try, for example, taking notes from a documentary so that your eyes alternate between the screen and your writing pad), one may experience being pulled between the beta/analytical and the alpha viewing state. Such experiments involve what Krugman calls 'resistance' to the 'basic electrical response of the brain to the medium'.

Most viewing does not encourage conscious attention. We are tired, wish to relax, and the effort of critical attention is not worth it. In any case, Marshall McLuhan maintained that the 'response to the medium may well be at the level of the nervous system, working its larger effect regardless of critical analysis on the part of the viewer'.[12]

What are the implications for children?

The implications for young children of the TV/Brain phenomenon are far reaching. Firstly, they are far more impressionable than the adults in Krugman's research. As we have seen, they are wide open to electronic images, and therefore to the 'spaced-out' state the medium induces. Secondly, if the electronic media do indeed inhibit the decision-making area of the brain, then children may simply be unable to switch off – with the implication that parents will then need to switch off the set for their children. Thirdly, the pace of the imagery and electronic scanning 'glues' eyes to the tube.

How do the electronic media affect the development of children's senses and the brain?

A child's brain develops from the basic core, action, or reptilian brain, to the limbic, old mammalian, or feeling brain, to the thought brain or neocortex. There are sensitive 'windows' in brain development when the stimulus, such as conversation with parents, must be present for the capacity of, say, language to develop. Young brains are also very plastic, with the potential for making vast numbers of dendritic connections. This fades at 10–11 years of age, so adults have to work much harder to make new connections.

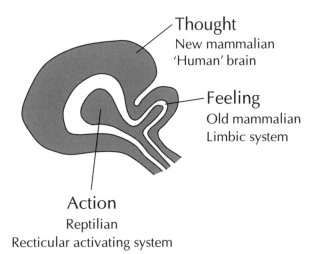

Figure 1   Source: Pearce, Joseph Chilton, *Evolution's End: Claiming the Potential of Our Intelligence*, Harper Collins: San Francisco, 1992.

The *action* brain processes sense impressions, controls movements, monitors body functions, manages reflexes, and helps our physical survival. The limbic, *feeling* brain responds with 'fight or flight' to threats, so humans react emotionally and physically before we have time to think in a crisis.[13]

The limbic brain enfolds the action brain (see Figure 1), processing emotional information such as likes and dislikes. It gives meaning to our experiences and learning, influencing behaviour and intimate relationships. It allows us to dream, fantasize, and experience intuitions and feelings, stimulated by the neocortex or thinking brain. The feeling brain is a bridge between the thought brain and the action brain – so in an emergency the action brain takes over the higher functions. A feature of the action and feeling brains is that they are unable to distinguish between a real or an imagined sense impression – hence they react first, and think later.

The neocortex or thought brain takes time to develop – it is five times the size of the other two brains combined. Its tasks are thinking, intellect, creativity, and calculation. The thinking brain receives sensory input from the action and feeling brains, but needs time to process information. The thinking brain is the vehicle for our experiences, perceptions, memories, feelings, and thinking, so we can form our ideas and actions.

The child's brain is progressively mylenated, in a process that begins with the action brain and ends with the neocortex. Mylenation covers the nerve dendrites and axons with a protective sheath of fatty acids. The more the nerve pathways are used, the more they are mylenated. The thicker the sheath, the faster the nerve impulse travels along the pathways. So young children's motor sensory pathways and senses need stimulation for mylenation to occur – e.g. as in rhythm games and movement.

The senses need stimulating and nurturing, but they also require protection from over- or inappropriate stimulation, as young children are like sponges (cf. Chapter 3). It takes time to develop the capacity for screening out unpleasant sense experiences, as young children are receptive to what they hear, see, touch, smell, and taste. So just consider the extent to which the electronic media are over-stimulating for children's delicate senses, and how the TV/Brain phenomenon works even more strongly with children than with adults.

The Reticular Activating System (or RAS) of the lower brain develops with the senses. The RAS is the focus and gateway of the different sense impressions, so that they are co-ordinated and can then be processed by the thought brain. The RAS enables us to give attention, to focus awareness, so that if the motor sensory pathways are poorly developed, this may lead to children having short attention spans and a poor ability to concentrate. Too much or too little stimulation of the senses, together with underdeveloped fine and gross motor skills, can lead to poor attention.

The action and feeling brains are 80 per cent mylenated by the age of 4. Brain development at 6–7 then moves on to the thought brain, the neocortex, with mylenation starting first on the right hemisphere, and then on the left. The right side helps process images, shapes, patterns, and sees the picture rather than the detail. It is more intuitive, and is active in art, music, and colour. As the right brain responds to colour and novelty, it therefore becomes dominant when watching TV.

The left hemisphere leads when a child thinks, reads, writes, and speaks. It underpins analysis, sequential thinking, and step-by-step logic, later developing into the abstract thinking needed in science. When learning to read, the left brain helps to connect the letters of the alphabet to the sounds and the meaning.

As children develop, the two hemispheres develop interconnections via the corpus callosum. This is a large bundle of nerve pathways which acts as a bridge, helping the co-ordination of the left and right sides of the body. The mylenation of the corpus callosum is helped by the development of gross motor skills – so running, exercises, singing games, jumping, and so on are all helpful here. The fine motor skills are also important for mylenation, with crafts, cooking, knitting, drawing, and painting. Such activities facilitate the development of flexibility, creativity, playing with ideas, imagination, and the interaction of intuitive and analytical thinking. The impaired development of the corpus callosum could affect the healthy interaction of the two hemispheres and could therefore be a cause of learning difficulties.[14]

Box 5

Games Stunt Teen Brains

'Computer games are creating a dumbed-down generation of children far more disposed to violence than their parents, according to a controversial new study. The tendency to lose control is not due to children absorbing the aggression involved in the computer game itself, as previous researchers have suggested, but rather to the damage done by stunting the developing mind.

Using the most sophisticated technology available, the level of brain activity was measured in hundreds of teenagers playing a Nintendo game and compared with the brain scans of other students doing a simple, repetitive arithmetical exercise. To the surprise of brain-mapping expert Professor Ryuta Kawashima and his team at Tohoku University in Japan, it was found that the computer game only stimulated activity in the areas of the brain associated with vision and movement.

In contrast, arithmetic stimulated brain activity in both the left and the right hemispheres of the frontal lobe – the brain most associated with learning, memory, and emotion.

Most worrying of all was that the frontal lobe, which continues to develop in humans until the age of about 20, also has an important role to play in keeping an individual's behaviour in check …

The students who played computer games were halting the process of brain development and affecting their ability to control potentially anti-social elements in their behaviour.

"The importance of this discovery cannot be underestimated", Kawashima told the *Observer*.'

Tracy McVeigh, *Observer* (London),
19 August 2001.

Kawashima had originally expected that his research would be a boon to the video game makers, who funded this work, and to parents who needed reassurance about the benefits of their children playing computer games. However, he concluded that arithmetic, reading, playing outside with other children, and conversation is better for child development and creativity than the playing of computer games.

To summarize, then, children mylenate their neural pathways by using their brains. A rich sensory diet and healthy movement help build flexible, strong neural connections – the more connections, the better. When a toddler is playing with her food, for example, she can taste, smell, and move the food around, then drop her plate on to the floor to gauge reactions and initiate a conversation. All the time, neural, dendritic connections are being made, so that when children play (for example, with a ball or bricks), they are setting millions of interconnecting neurons into play. Healthy movement, repetition, play, conversation, and multi-sensory stimulation are essential for the development of the brain.

How do the electronic media affect the senses and brains of young children?

In the process of discovering the world, young children are faced with the problem of 'sensing' whether television and computer pictures are 'real' or not. *Is* there, in fact, a man in the box? How is the virtual reality of the screen world different from the real world that can be touched, tasted, smelt? Reports of tribal people's responses to films – of being very concerned about where the actor has gone once he leaves the screen – demonstrate the initial confusion that technology can precipitate. You can imagine how puzzling television may be to children who are just becoming aware of the differences and variety of sensory experience. My 3-year-old son once asked, 'Is there really an orchestra in the box?', and 'Is that man really dead?'

Television is a deceptive medium to which to expose young children as they are learning to find their way in the everyday world. Consider the contrast between live puppets and a show produced on the TV screen. The live performance holds children spellbound: they can see the puppets and enter the 'make-believe' world of the story in which they become totally engaged and immersed. Television, on the other hand, projects a vast number of images, people, and happenings that are second-hand reproductions of things taking place at a distance. Furthermore, many events happening on the screen – the technical tricks, the cartoon antics, all the artificial unusualness used to attract the viewer – cannot take place in real life. So young children are faced with a 'real world' which they need to get used to through the normal development of the senses, and an electronic world where events happen which are unknown and often 'impossible' in everyday life.

A mother described an incident with her 5-year-old stepdaughter whom she described as a tele-addict:

'About six months ago she ran into the road and was hit by a car, and fortunately escaped with one bruise and shock. A few hours after the accident she asked me what had happened and I explained, telling her that she was a very lucky girl. I asked, "What would have happened if you had fallen under the wheels?", and she answered, "I'd jump up again like the Pink Panther!"'

One father, on taking his young son to the zoo, was so concerned by comments like 'I've already seen all this on television!' that he got rid of the television altogether. Reality, he concluded, cannot compete with a box that shows close-ups of tigers, lions, and rhinos, scenes which one never meets in ordinary life in such rapid succession. He also felt that television was dulling his child's sense of wonder.

The electronic media and sight

The electronic media also affect our sense of sight. The eye responds to colour, light, and darkness, on the one hand, and to movement on the other. In fact, movement and balance – two other distinct senses (see Chapter 5) – are intimately connected with the eye. One's eye is in continual movement, busy gauging distance, height, and depth, which are in turn the essential elements of perspective. The eyes are perpetually fixing objects in their vision, accommodating and shifting their focus. It takes time to learn how to perceive objects: for example, a 2 year old will only again recognize a triangle that has been rotated 120 degrees when he has also rotated his head; so visual exploration is therefore a prerequisite of seeing. In fact, children's visual acuity and full binocular or three-dimensional vision are only developed fully by the age of 4.

Research evidence is increasingly demonstrating the damaging effects of the screen culture on children's eye sight. In a recent feature article, journalist Tim Utton, quoting Adrian Knowles of the Eyecare Trust charity, writes that 'Experts believe modern living – particularly time spent in front of the TV and computer screens – is damaging the eyesight of increasing numbers of youngsters' – with the advice that 'All children should have an eye examination before they are three, while everyone should have their eyes tested every two years.'[15]

How does television affect babies' and toddlers' developing sense of sight? The perceptual world is not a finished product (this being so for all of us), but rather, it is shaped according to a person's age. Children's experiences happen in a vivid world in which things are attractive and repulsive before they focus into abstract qualities like squareness or blackness. Psychologist Jean Piaget showed how optical illusions decrease with age, and how children's perception of space develops. For the first few months, objects do not 'exist' if they are not moving or doing something. Holding or manipulating an object gives it reality, and when it disappears, it is gone for good. Space, like 'mouth space' or 'grasping space', is separate and related to activity.

At the 8th–10th month, the object is seen to be more independent. Piaget offered a watch to a 9 month old who then played with it. When it was hidden under a pillow, the baby fetched it. Even though the baby saw the watch being hidden in a different place the second time, he still looked in the first hiding place.

At about 16 months, the toddler perceives the object as having permanence independent of himself. Space becomes a field in which things happen, as opposed to being bound up with activity. Perhaps the game of 'peek-a-boo' is a way for babies and toddlers to get used to seeing loved ones come and go, yet still feeling they are 'there'. The sense of sight continues to develop, and it is only at around the age of 11–12 that the sense for perspective emerges. From the standpoint of perceptual development, therefore, television may seriously harm the acquiring of concepts like space by infants. Moreover, the two-dimensional screen inhibits the development of a sense of depth and perspective.

In adults, perception is dependent on all kinds of exploratory eye movements, from consciously directed ones to involuntary small ones which shift the image over the fovea when the eye seems fixated on a motionless object. Interestingly, in the context of television's effects on the eye, when such scanning motions are artificially suppressed, the image breaks up into fragments. We need to 'finger over the visual field with our gaze', as one physiologist observed. Constant eye movement is required for a healthy eye. Lack of eye movement may be a symptom of ageing, and eye specialists can give exercises to help older people keep their eyes 'young'.

For focusing, we need conscious attention, vigilance, and concentration; in short, we have to exert ourselves to co-operate with the faculties this sense provides for us.

Attention is needed for good observation and focalization. Attention is a condition which has a real opposite in the confused, dazed, 'scatter-brained state' which in French is called 'distraction'. Such attention requires effort.

Television-watching is a visually passive activity. One's head is stationary, the eyes are practically motionless and do not continually move to get 'fixes' on objects, as they do in normal sight. They are slightly 'defocused' to take in the whole screen. The accent is on peripheral vision rather than on central vision, which is active in the state of attention described above. Another effect is that, whilst watching television, one's eye muscles are not being exercised and one's vigilance is decreased through the necessary defocusing of the eyes. There is little need for accommodating eye movement – or rather, this is kept at a constant level to make up for the nature of the CRT, which is a slightly blurred, low-definition medium. (Compare the electronic images with the clearer images of cinema films, for example.) Some ophthalmologists recommend TV viewing for post-operative eye patients, just to keep the eyes stilled.

Good visual skills are needed for reading. Reading requires developed eye muscles, so as to enable the eyes' saccadic movement, when the eyes jump or focus on groups of words and move jerkily from line to line. Reading also requires focus and attention, which are reduced by viewing. Whilst watching a tele-screen, children's eyes tend not to blink, dilate, and show little eye movement. Pupil dilation and tracking are integrated by the reticular activating system (RAS). The RAS helps guide what is attended to, and relates to children's ability to focus and concentrate, so if this is poorly integrated with the neocortex or thought brain, then reading and thinking are affected.

How can you tell if your brain integration is breaking down? What you might notice if you have been working on screen for a while is an increasing number of spelling mistakes, getting to the end of a line and losing the thread of an argument, or fatigue. Charles Krebs, a scientist and chiropractor, thinks that people have varying levels of brain integration; but even those with excellent brain integration can become disoriented by long exposure to the screen:

'People with poor brain integration and learning problems are the most susceptible ... Often such children will sit in front of the television before they go to school. At school, they sit under fluorescent lights all day (another factor that may cause loss of integration), and when they return home, they once again sit in front of the television. *These children are in a constant state of environmentally generated brain disintegration.*'[16]

Krebs then told the story of a New Zealand teacher who asked their class of 7 year olds to sign a week-long contract not to watch television. According to the teacher, and the children, they reported they could work better as a result.

Finally, one key feature of the senses and the lower brain is that the visual stimulus takes first place over the auditory stimulus or sound. We instinctively trust our sight more. 'Seeing is believing', but it is *not* the case that 'hearing is believing'. Thus, for example, a group of 6–7 year olds were shown a video in which the sound track did not match the images and action. When questioned, the children did not register the mismatch – they had focused on the pictures, not the sounds.[17]

Box 6

Kids' Eyesight in Peril: Computers 'May Cause Permanent Damage'

'Millions of children who regularly use computers may suffer permanent damage to their eyes, a controversial new study has claimed. Researchers say almost one in three children could develop short-sightedness unless they wear specifically prescribed glasses.

They add that when many people scan a piece of text on screen, they mistakenly focus slightly beyond the words. The eye muscles have to work hard to quickly refocus. The strain of the effort can start headaches and is suspected of causing lasting damage. For the first time, scientists at the American Optometric Association have found a significant link between the time children spend at their computers, and the extent of their mis-focusing. They have concluded that staring at screens does put children at risk of becoming short-sighted.

Researcher Cary Herzberg told *New Scientist* magazine that children who use computers should be tested to see if they need special glasses. Mr Herzberg, an optometrist in Aurora, Illinois, said, "As children spend more time on the computer and at other near-point tasks, their risk of developing myopia increases. We are definitely seeing more children now with this type of problem than we did five years ago.'"

Michael Leventhal, Science Editor, *Daily Express*, 12 April 2002

Children just don't seem to listen any more ...

Kindergarten teachers are saying that they are increasingly having to teach children to listen. Although most children love stories, their attention span seems shorter, and a minority find it difficult to listen at all. However, as soon as such children begin to make their own inner gesture-like 'pictures' of the story, they *are* then able to listen. Little surprise, then, that teachers are commenting upon how much better story-tellers they need to be nowadays to hold children's attention.

One cause could be that the background noise of radio, video, or television in the home is so prevalent that the sense of hearing is being dulled. Since television is more visual than aural, and unless adults converse with children and tell them stories, children's sense of hearing is not being fully exercised. One piece of research showed that, 25 years ago, the average person could distinguish between 300,000 sounds; today that figure is just 180,000, reflecting a pronounced and ongoing attenuation of the brain's sensitivity.

Dr Sally Ward, a speech and language therapist, was so struck by the observation of the growing numbers of children attending her clinic with delayed language, and the comment 'Children don't seem to listen any more', that she conducted extensive research over ten years into what was happening in the home. Research into a thousand children in Manchester found that no less than *one in five pre-school children had listening and attention problems* that delayed their language development. Incidence doubled between 1984 and 1990, coinciding with the extension of breakfast and daytime television. 'With the most severely affected ones, people suspected that they were profoundly deaf. But they're not deaf, they're switched off, they haven't been able to develop the ability to listen selectively.'[18]

Ward frankly found her findings 'frightening', observing how television had come to dominate relationships between parents and children:

> 'It's a whole change in culture, people don't interact with children in the way that they used to. People used to have three-piece suites arranged at conversational distance. They are now all in a line facing the telly, and you see kids in a darkened room just with the television.'[19]

Many parents leave the TV on all the time, for 'company' and to keep the children occupied. During the first few crucial months, babies are commonly unable to hear their parents talking above the noise. Moreover, this is occurring at the critical stage when babies need one-to-one contact with their parents so as to distinguish the meaningful sounds of their parents' speech from meaningless background noise. Ward again:

'Children are focusing exclusively on the noise from televisions and stereos, and ignoring the sound of human voices. Consequently learning to speak is delayed and other social and educational problems arise. In some homes I visited, constant noise came from more than one source – two television sets or a television and a stereo. Adults can block out unwanted background and foreground noise but young children do not have this ability. Babies need a big difference in background noise in order to focus on someone speaking.'

At eight months, then, many of the babies in the study neither recognized their own names nor basic words like 'juice' and 'bricks'. Nor is this phenomenon confined to inner city Manchester, where the original research was done, for Ward is increasingly finding middle-class parents allowing the electronic media to dominate their homes:

'The television is being used as a babysitter, with nannies particularly. Some of these middle class children are spending far too much time watching television and videos. They get very fixed on colours and flashing lights. They are riveted by the screen. We found in our study that it was quite difficult to get them interested in toys.'[20]

Some children have very little language at two years. 'I have seen children of two and a half with virtually no ability to understand words.' Sometimes, they cannot speak at all, only being able to make gulping noises, which Ward puts down to early over-exposure to television. Also undermined are children's abilities to listen, to learn, to take turns in a conversation, reading facial expressions, and telling when the other person has finished talking. For example, Ward describes a victim of early exposure: 'He comes into the room and ploughs right past you. If you put a box of toys on the floor he ploughs through that too, wandering rather aimlessly around and looking at nobody and nothing.'[21]

Observational skills may also not be developed by television-viewing – hence the need to help children see flowers, animals, and birds. Many infant, Kindergarten, and junior teachers whom I know have observed a 'withdrawal' from the senses in moderate-and heavy-viewing children. They therefore need to teach therapeutically so as to cultivate the ability to 'see a world in a grain of sand'.

Movement and balance

Some older teachers can still distinguish the 'viewers' from the 'non-viewers' in a class, by their posture, movement, limb control, and how they sit. Audrey McAllen, a special education advisor, wrote on movement and television:

'After many years of working with children who have learning difficulties I can see how unconnected the present-day child is with the interaction of hands and limbs. They do not bother to lift their legs high enough to throw a ball under them, the hand collides with the thigh. Also the left leg seems heavier than the right and harder for them to lift. When classes have been screened for learning problems, this symptom of limb heaviness is now general among children.'[22]

You can experience this 'limb heaviness' for yourself after watching TV. Perhaps this is why there are currently so many popular types of movement class for adults such as Tai Chi or yoga: to counteract the effects of computer work and our sedentary lifestyle.

According to Aeppli,[23] the human sense of movement works very precisely, perceiving the very finest movements taking place in our physical body. Moreover, every movement we make with the body is an expression of the will. The movement sense gives us the feeling of having a reason to be here, a sense of purpose developed from wanting to go from one place to another. The sense of movement also enables us, through our muscles, to perceive if we are still or moving, and where our body is located in space. Young children subtly imitate the movements in their environment, resonating, for example, to electronic movements. Learning to walk, and to develop dexterity and co-ordination, all relate to the sense of movement.

It comes as no surprise, therefore, that the limiting of movement through sedentary TV and computer use has profoundly disruptive effects. Consider, for example, hyperactivity, so-called 'attention deficit disorder', and forms of dyslexia when letters move up and down in the visual field. Dr Harry Levinson treats certain forms of dyslexia and hyperactivity with travel sickness pills. These children, he believes, suffer from a kind of 'motion sickness'. Certain children's ability to read increases remarkably after taking these pills, because the disturbed sense of movement is stabilized.[24]

Alan Hall, a physicist investigating electromagnetic fields, noticed the effects of rapidly oscillating, low-level electromagnetic fields coming from computers and televisions: 'When one comes within two feet or 18 inches, one can feel the muscles tighten up slightly, and over time a feeling of "electrostress".' As a result he suggests considering how such subtle oscillations can affect balance and movement in young children, drawing upon your own direct experience.[25]

Balance is also affected by TV-watching. How many times do adults say they want to find balance in their lives! Balance is centred in the inner ear, sensing the pull of the earth; it gives us a sense of uprightness. It gives us a bodily, grounded reference point, a feeling of inner calm, and security in space. Consider, in this context, the modern dizzy pace of life[26] and how this can knock us off balance …

The achieving of balance is a major accomplishment for infants, as well as that of standing upright, rendering the child free to start moving as an independent being in the world. Cheryl Sanders stresses that balance disorders, resulting from activities like TV-viewing, can have devastating effects upon children:

'The disruption of balance causes a certain sinking feeling in the stomach, a dizziness that might be familiar to spinning about ten or twelve times, then trying to walk straight. Imagine if this feeling were present every time you wanted to read, or write. What if the feeling were more subtle, so that you could not figure out what it was, but you knew you were feeling awful when at school, especially in some classes, but not in others like art or music ... and what if lack of co-ordination was extended to any attempt to participate in games, or even just trying to run across the playground without being laughed at?'[27]

In a Nutshell ...

1. TV, video, the Internet, and computer games are here to stay. The electronic media offer entertainment, communication, education, and information – as well as useful tools for work. However, because the cathode-ray tube is such a useful and powerful machine, with a range of negative side-effects that work-places recognize and guard against, the question is, 'How appropriate is the CRT for children under seven?'
2. The CRT used by the electronic media is a powerful machine that overloads and 'tunes out' the brain. This can damage young children's brains, which are sensitive, and attuned to learning from real life and people.
3. The CRT has been linked with many kinds of learning difficulty such as attention 'disorders', hyperactivity, poor memory, lack of concentration, the need for instant gratification, short attention spans, impulsive behaviour, movement difficulties, and poor listening and language skills.
4. Media content and programming is geared to hold children's attention, so that they find it hard to walk away from them. Children therefore need adults' help with switching off.

5. *Physical Hazards II*

Light and Movement Injuries

In this chapter, two further sources of physical health hazards are investigated: viz. the effects of television light, and the various movement injuries (i.e. repetitive strain and musculo-skeletal injuries) that arise from computer use.

Television Light and Health

Light affects us so profoundly that researchers have looked into how light influences health. In northern countries, for example, where people are prone to seasonal affective disorder or SAD, natural spectrum artificial lighting systems have been developed to counter people developing the winter blues. So how does the CRT light affect babies and children?

Children are highly sensitive to light, and infants are like sense organs that touch, taste, and feel the world with their whole being (cf. Chapter 3). A toddler will quiver with delight at seeing a beloved object, a baby will taste the warmth and goodness of milk 'all over his body', or respond to a sound with his whole organism. One of the first experiences babies have is of light, and of being caressed by light all over their bodies.

Just as food nourishes the metabolism, and air nourishes the lungs with oxygen, so light feeds people. Babies need light, especially daylight, a 'food', in order to thrive. The nourishing effects of light were discovered when babies with jaundice were observed to recover more quickly near to windows than they did in darker parts of dormitories. Light is now given as a successful therapy for neonatal jaundice. Light – whether daylight, blue light, or full spectrum white light of a reasonable level – effectively reduces the bilirubin levels, which are out of balance.

Rickets in infants is caused by a lack of vitamin D, which is produced in the skin of the body with the help of daylight. This used to be more of a problem in industrial areas where a large percentage of daylight was screened out by air pollution. One cure is to take infants outside, to expose them to light.

Care for the 'light environment' of babies is therefore of great importance. Dr Frederic Leboyer, for example, recommends that lights be dimmed during childbirth, and that the newly born be protected from bright lights. Over the first few weeks of life, babies should sleep in darkened rooms and be introduced slowly to daylight and to artificial light. This gives the delicate, sensitive eyes of babies the chance to become accustomed to light.

Leboyer underlines the 'sharpness and freshness' of the unorganized senses of newly born babies, and how overwhelming their perceptions of the world are. These infantile perceptions make the senses of adults look pale in comparison. He writes:

'The baby has the same love, the same thirst for light that plants and flowers have. The baby is passionate about light, drunk with it. So much so, that we should offer it more slowly, with endless precautions. In fact, babies are so sensitive to light that they perceive it while still in the mother's womb. If a mother more than six months' pregnant is naked in sunlight, the baby within her sees it as a golden haze. And now this small creature, so sensitive to light, is suddenly thrust out of its dark lair, and eyes are exposed to floodlights. It screams, and not surprisingly … If our aim were to drive it mad with pain, we couldn't go about it better. The poor baby squeezes its eyes shut. But what help is the fragile, transparent barrier of its eyelids? The truth is that the new born baby is not blind, but blinded.'[1]

The light researcher Dr John Ott questioned whether the excessive absorption of artificial light could affect people physically. It was Ott's work that had an influence on the substantial reduction in the amount of X-rays emitted from television sets.[2]

Television light is projected into our eyes by cathode ray guns behind the screen, powered by 25,000 kilovolts in colour sets, and 18,000 kilovolts in black and white sets. These guns shoot streams of electrons at the phosphor dots on the screen, which in turn beam light into the viewer's eyes. This directed light is projected *into* the viewer, rather than the viewer looking *at* the lighted screen.

Such light has concrete physical effects on organisms. The retina registers the light stimuli and on the one hand translates these into images, which are carried to the brain. At the same time, light rays permeate through neurochemical pathways the pineal and pituitary glands and then into the endocrine systems. The light thus 'nourishes' the organism biochemically. An analogy here is the plant which fixes energy directly out of light by means of photosynthesis. It is only gradually that babies become used to the cycle of day and night to which their waking and sleeping rhythm becomes adjusted.

The change from a diet of natural light to a diet of predominantly artificial light has resulted in 'malillumination'. We get 'overdoses' of incandescent, fluorescent, and television light, whereas we are 'starved' of natural light.

Malillumination may result in complaints such as lowered vitality, less resistance to disease, and hyperactivity. It may also contribute to aggressive behaviour, heart illness, and cancer.[3]

Ott became interested in the effects of television radiation and light through reading about why children get tired.[4] Two air-force doctors had found that the common symptoms of headaches, nerves, bad sleep patterns, vomiting, and general fatigue amongst a group of 30 children were related to their watching television from three to six hours on week days, and six to ten hours at weekends.

The doctors suggested that the children stop watching, and in 12 cases where this advice was followed, the symptoms disappeared within just three weeks. In 18 cases, viewing time was limited to two hours daily and the symptoms faded away in five or six weeks. In the 11 cases where the rules were relaxed after the initial period, the children watched as much as before and the previous symptoms returned.[5]

To test the hypothesis that such symptoms were caused by television radiation, Ott put six pots – each containing three bean seeds – in front of a colour television screen half-covered with a black photographic paper which would stop all visible light. Six pots were put in front of the other half of the screen, which was shielded with lead, whilst a control of six pots was placed 50 feet away.

After three weeks, the lead-shielded and the outdoor beans showed 6 inches of normal growth. The beans subjected to radiation, showed an excessive vine-type growth ranging up to 31½ inches. Furthermore, the leaves were all approximately 2½ to 3 times the size of those of the outdoor plants and those protected by the lead shielding.

A similar experiment was conducted on rats. The rats shielded by black paper alone 'became increasingly hyperactive and aggressive within from three to ten days, and then became progressively lethargic. At thirty days they were extremely lethargic and it was necessary to push them to make them move about the cage'. Those rats behind the lead shielding showed much milder abnormal symptoms, which also took much longer to develop.

Perhaps Ott's most important work in this context was on fluorescent light, since the CRT is fluorescent. He discovered that different forms of light had marked effects on the streaming of the chloroplasts – the forming movement of cells within plants. Whilst subjected to sunlight a rhythmical pattern would be maintained, but with different fluorescents the pattern changed dramatically.

The next experimental step was to subject cancer-sensitive mice to different lights. An experiment with 300 such mice showed a 61 per cent survival rate with pink fluorescent, 94 per cent with white fluorescent, 88 per cent with all fluorescents, and 97 per cent for ordinary daylight.

Whilst the effects of light on natal jaundice and rickets are known, there is less experimental evidence about the effects of CRT-light on people. Dr Richard J. Wurtman of the Massachusetts Institute of Technology wrote a paper in the *Scientific American* on the effects of artificial light. Whilst agreeing with Ott that the body may be radically influenced by different light spectra, Wurtman concluded:

'Both government and industry have been satisfied to allow people who buy electric lamps – first the incandescent ones and now the fluorescent – to serve as the unwitting subjects in a long-term experiment on the effects of artificial lighting environments on human health. We have been lucky, perhaps, in that so far the experiment has had no demonstrably baneful effects.'[6]

So is television light harmful to children's health? Since babies and children are highly sensitive to light, exposure to fluorescent and TV light certainly needs to be strictly limited. For babies and toddlers there is certainly no better light diet than daylight or sunlight.

Electromagnetic radiation

The development of the CRT (VDT) has resulted in higher and higher radiation protection standards, yet despite this, Ott argued that low-level electromagnetic radiation given off might have effects without showing any visible damage. Electromagnetic radiation (or EMR) is the radiation given off by electrical appliances and wiring, as well as power lines. Every time you switch on an appliance, you are fluxed by EMR. Whilst EMRs are thought not to cause serious health effects, some researchers think that even low-level fields can cause stress in our bodies and brains. The US National Council on Radiation Protection was concerned that 'There was a powerful body of impressive evidence to suggest that very low exposures to EMRs has subtle, long-term effects on human health.'[7]

The continual flux of electromagnetic radiation is one reason why people experience fatigue when they are working on-screen for long periods, and it also explains why many people fall asleep in front of the TV. Those affected by EMRs find that exposure disorients them so that their brain escapes the stress by going to sleep.

Box 7

TV Health Tips

Many mains-powered electrical devices give off radiation from electromagnetic fields. There are concerns about the possible links between EMR and cancer, effects on the brain and on the nervous system.

Tips:

- Sit more than six feet from the screen, as EMR declines with distance.
- The back of TV sets can emit high EMR.
- TVs even give off radiation when not switched on – so switch them off at the mains and also save energy.
- There are many protection devices for countering EMR.

However, it also depends on the individual: some people are so highly sensitive to EMRs that they experience pain. One person, for example, found the TV so painful that he arranged a series of mirrors to reflect the pictures into another room, thus allowing him to watch in comfort.

There is, however, a wide range of individual responses to EMRs, with some people not experiencing any effects. One test you can try for yourself is to pay attention to your body's reactions when you gradually approach a TV or computer. Just pay attention to what your body feels. When I tried this with a computer, for example, I noticed a slight tension appearing in my muscles on getting within two feet of a computer. Some people commonly report that computer work creates physical tension, though there may be various causes of which EMRs could be one factor. EMR effects, again depending on the person, can also be demonstrated using kinesiology or muscle testing, according to Dr Charles Krebs, who calls the effects of EMRs 'electrostress'. He writes that these can affect your brain integration and energy balance:

'If you have good brain integration and your body is energetically balanced, you will have strong resistance to these electromagnetic perturbations. But if you have poor brain integration, the constant flux of electromagnetic energy can cause a distortion of your energetic body, which can then cause mental confusion and other physiological effects such as fatigue. Even in people who have good brain integration, long exposures to these fields can cause a breakdown in mental function and fatigue.'[8]

Symptoms of the loss of brain integration include starting to make spelling mistakes, losing the thread of what you are writing, and tiredness.

Krebs emphasizes that in the modern world, it is hard to avoid fluorescent lighting, TVs, and computers. He suggests that, in the face of this electromagnetic onslaught, brain integration can be maintained by protective devices and by balancing the body's energetic systems using kinesiology or brain gym.[9] (See Appendix 3: Movement, Health and Ergonomic Tips for Computer Use.) However, the human response to EMRs is like the various responses to allergens – only people who are electromagnetically sensitive will experience harm from normal exposure.

Toxic emissions

There are 21 chemicals in the emissions of new CRTs, taking up to 360 hours to dissipate. In computer rooms at work-places, such emissions can result in skin, ear, nose, and throat irritations. Electromagnetic fields from CRTs are a possible cancer hazard, with much less protection at the sides and backs of sets. Newer sets are usually safer, and children should sit a reasonable distance – say three feet away from CRTs which are more than 5 years old.[10]

Repetitive Strain Injury (RSI) and Musculo-skeletal Injuries

'Childhood repetitive strain injuries: "It's probably a time bomb waiting to go off." '

Dr Margit Bleeker[11]

Computers are used extensively in many schools now, and even in infants' classes. One study found that students spent 16 hours a week using computers, and over 3 hours a day. RSI and carpel tunnel syndrome in adults have resulted in extensive work-place health and safety training, with ergonomic redesign. Yet in schools and at home this is often disregarded.

Box 8

Case Study

'Charlotte Cook, 14, says she has been suffering from severe neck pains since she started using computers for schoolwork four years ago. She spends at least one hour at her keyboard doing homework each evening and up to four hours at weekends. In addition, she uses computers at school to research essays on the internet. Charlotte receives treatment from a chiropractor every three months to contain the problem. On occasions the pain gets so bad she has to take a day off school.

Charlotte, of Godalming, Surrey, said, "I usually find that after a long piece of homework I get aches in my neck and my upper back, between my shoulders. I have to concentrate on how I am sitting, but it is not always easy because I am concentrating so much on the work I am doing."'

B Marsh and J Mills, *Daily Mail*, 28 November 2000

The constant repetition of a limited number of fine hand movements for typing, pointing, and clicking with a mouse can stress the hands, tendons, muscles, nerves, and bones of children still at a sensitive age. Indeed, the computer for young children is a kind of technological straitjacket for the body. Their bodies want to move, so sitting still at a screen goes against the grain.

Dr Leon Straker of Curtin University, Australia said that,

'This is the first generation of children who have used computers from childhood when their bones and muscles are developing. If we don't get knowledge quickly about how to use computers safely, then I think we will see a lot of children disabled from using computers.'[12]

Box 9

Computer Generation Face a Life of Pain

'One in three children will be left with permanent, painful injuries because of the hours they spend on computers, experts are warning. They fear that an epidemic of repetitive strain injury is looming among youngsters who spend hours at a time sitting in front of a screen using a keyboard or clicking a mouse. According to a study unveiled yesterday, 36 per cent of 11–14 year-olds suffer serious, ongoing back pain ... Little attention has been paid to [researching into the effects on] children. But today's youngsters are the first to have used computers from an early age, at which their muscles and bones are still developing.

Professor Peter Buckle, of the Robens Centre for Health Economics at the University of Surrey, described the findings of the study, involving more than 2,000 youngsters, as deeply alarming ...

Research suggests that those who do suffer from low back pain in school are very likely to face lifelong problems, the professor said ... Part of the problem, he told a conference, was that children were having to use computer equipment and furniture at school and at home that was designed to be used by adults ... [Most parents] seem unaware of the possible dangers of children sitting for long periods unsupported, with necks twisted and wrists over-extended. The professor suggested that classrooms should be subject to health and safety assessments ... [He] advised parents to monitor their children's computer use at home, making them take regular exercise and encouraging them to sit properly.'

Tim Utton, Science Reporter, *Daily Mail*, 10 September 2002, p. 15

In Australia, computers have been widely used in schools far longer than in Britain, and the problem is emerging. Dr Straker's study found that even 10 year olds were suffering chronic RSI pains. Children he surveyed were using computers for more than three hours a day, and had neck, back, shoulder, and head pains. He found problems in 60 per cent of the children using keyboards.

Laptops result in more risks of musculo-skeletal injuries than desktop computers, according to Allan Hedge of Cornell University. Poor posture and strain resulted from carrying laptops around as keyboard and monitor are attached, and students were either straining the necks because the monitor was too low, or their wrists because the keyboard was too high. The advice for older children was to take a break every 20 minutes, and no more than three quarters of any hour in front of the computer screen.

Box 10

How Children of Today Face a Life of Back Pain

'Hours of sitting in front of computer screens and carrying heavy school bags around are condemning children to a lifetime of back pain, according to research [by the British Chiropractic Association] … The association … says modern children are more at risk from developing joint and back pain than ever before … Some 38 per cent of parents estimate their children spend more than five hours a week playing computer games or using a PC …

Computer use should be limited to periods of not more than 40 minutes at a time, while sitting comfortably and with support for the spine … The situation for children is now so serious that back checks should become as routine for them as going to the dentist, said the BCA … Tim Hutchful of the association said: "Children are extremely vulnerable to back

> problems later in life, as their young bones are soft and still developing ... Our research highlighted how worried parents are." ...
>
> A study by doctors in Finland, published in the *British Medical Journal* this month, found an alarming increase in the incidence of pain in the neck, shoulders and lower back among adolescents between 1991 and 2001. The study found that among girls, 24 per cent of 14-year-olds, 38 per cent of 16-year-olds and 45 per cent of 18-year-olds had upper back problems. The doctors, from the University of Tampere, suggested that increased computer use was to blame.'
>
> Tim Utton, Science Reporter, *Daily Mail,* 21 October 2002, p. 19

Childhood obesity, lack of exercise, and movement disorders

There now exists the most sedentary generation of children in history – with childhood obesity levels rising dramatically and fitness levels falling. With obesity comes the increased risk of childhood diabetes. As many as one in ten children under the age of 4 is obese, from junk, high-fat, sugary food, lack of exercise, and sedentary TV/computer-dominated lifestyles. A third of adults are also overweight, risking more heart disease, diabetes, and high blood pressure. Children who view for more than four hours a day are significantly heavier that those viewing for less than two hours.[13]

The health risk from the rising number of 'couch potatoes' has prompted high-profile actions. In January 2001, for example, British Olympic stars Steve Redgrave and Denise Lewis started to tour youth clubs and schools up and down Great Britain to encourage young people to watch less television and to exercise more. The government also proposed extensive after-school physical education provision to raise fitness levels amongst school children.

Lack of exercise also undermines education and learning, as movement is essential for healthy learning. Movement activates the mind and the body, enabling us to integrate and embed new information. Phyllis Weikart is a child development expert who is concerned that children's bodily and movement needs have been overlooked by a one-sided focus on cognitive development. She observes that children today engage in up to 75 per cent less physical activity than they did in 1900:

'Children aren't playing, and through play a great deal of active learning takes place. Children used to play in natural ways, with kids of different ages, outside, basically unsupervised by adults. Visual and auditory attention, body co-ordination – all was gained through that kind of play. *This physical learning must take place before children start dealing with abstractions*; it doesn't happen if children don't have those experiences. Children are not encouraged to spend as much time crawling, or exploring their physical environment as they once were. We have children who are not growing up with adequate co-ordination. As a result there is much clumsiness in children … The body is the primary learning center for the child. We give inadequate attention to the body, so we are not building the foundations in developmentally appropriate ways.'[14]

Child development specialists note the connection between clumsiness and learning difficulties, pointing to the crucial role of movement for children. Movement activates physical, sensory, and intellectual growth; and children whose physical movement is restricted may suffer blocked or delayed growth of *apparently* unrelated faculties such as the ability to comprehend concepts. 'Every time we move in an organized, graceful manner, full brain activation and integration occurs, and the door to learning opens naturally', according to Carla Hannaford. So *we learn with the whole body*, rather than with just a disembodied brain. 'I do, and I understand', as the Chinese say.[15]

One story that illustrates the connection between movement and learning is that of Robin Smith who came to Ruskin Mill Further Education Centre at the age of 16. His constitutional tendency to a weakened spine led to a computer-induced stoop, after spending years addicted to playing *Game Boy*. 'His computer addiction was partly a defence against the extreme trauma of his abandonment by his family', said Aonghus Gordon of Ruskin Mill:

> 'He believed he was in a moving virtual world, and was totally caught up in this powerful hyper-kinetic screen activity of playing games. He believed he was being active, but in reality he was physically sedentary at the computer for hours. Yet at the same time he was caught up in soul wrenching, distorted pictures of heroism, electronic light, and rapid-fire images that pulverized his soul and depleted his energy. The result was that Robin developed a fixed stoop from gazing at close quarters into the screen.'

The remedy? Aonghus Gordon got Robin moving again by engaging his will and interest in a number of activities such as the craft of glass-blowing, coached by a master craftsman in this challenging, skilful craft. Instead of using the glass cathode-ray tube for computer games, Robin learned the careful hand/eye co-ordination and movements needed to shape molten glass so as to make beautiful glass works of art for other people. He has become a competent glass blower and is proud to demonstrate his skills. This was both invigorating and cathartic — a total change from an addiction to point-and-click with the mouse. An exciting development to this story is that Robin was involved in a project to recyle old CRTs for glass and lead.[16]

Box 11

Movement and Learning

Tai chi stretches a failing school into a big success

'The ancient Chinese art of Tai chi has turned a failing primary school round by enabling pupils to concentrate and improve their behaviour. Children as young as four have been learning the 1000-year-old therapeutic exercises since they were introduced after a damning inspection report. Each morning before lessons, the 56 pupils spend ten minutes on exercises that aim to integrate and relax the mind and body with a series of slow, rhythmic, and purposeful movements.

"Tai chi calms the children down and gets everyone in the right frame of mind", said Mrs Ellis, the Head. "Before school all the children are hyperactive and are running about ... After Tai chi they are very calm and relaxed and settled for class."'

Sarah Harris, *Daily Mail*, 13 October 2001

In a Nutshell ...

The effects of CRT (VDT) light, toxic emissions, low frequency EMRs, and the possibility of repetitive strain injury need to be monitored at home and in schools, with careful attention paid to ergonomics.

Rising levels of childhood obesity, lack of exercise, and movement disorders have been linked to excessive electronic media use. The inappropriate use of the electronic media in the early years is a major public health issue.

6. *Social Hazards of Screen Culture I*

Addiction, Play, Advertising, and Anti-social behaviour

'A lot of scared parents and a lot of trapped kids … '
Dr Sonia Livingstone, London School of Economics
and Political Science

The social, emotional, and behavioural effects of screen culture are, again, so pervasive, and the associated research so extensive, that it requires two separate chapters to consider them adequately. In this chapter, the effects upon addiction, children's play, advertising, and anti-social behaviour, including violence, are examined. Then, in Chapter 7 the cognitive and learning impacts upon children of an increasingly pervasive screen culture will be discussed.

The more screen culture takes hold, the less time there is for interaction and real conversation between children and parents. As children's bedrooms become ever more well equipped with the electronic media, they are spending increasing amounts of time plugged in – up to four or five hours a day. The number of face-to-face conversations and encounters is decreasing, as parents are spending less and less time with their children. Children are also leading more isolated lives, as families who are living together are, nonetheless, increasingly living separate lives. This retreat into an electronic world is also spurred by perceptions of a 'lean and mean' world which is hostile to children outside the home – where, for example, it is seen as being unsafe to play on the street or in the local park.

Dr Sonia Livingstone is researching the effects of the electronic media on children, in the course of which she has visited the homes of many British families. When asked what she found, she shook her head and said, 'A lot of scared parents and a lot of trapped kids.' She reported that 'Children seemed to be at their brightest and most confident when talking about going outside … A really boring day for most children meant watching television.' One parent said:

'I wouldn't dream of letting kids walk to school by themselves at that age [i.e. 11] nowadays. I would rather take him because there are so many funny people around. I mean, I'm sure that there were funny people years ago, but there were probably not so many of them.'[1]

Parents are thus filling their children's bedroom with the electronic media as a compensation or substitute for not being able to go out. She concludes that

'If we put together the particularly strong fears in Britain of the outdoors with the fact that British children are more likely [*sic*] to have a television in their bedroom of all children in Europe, we get a hint of the compensation that parents seem to be offering their children.'

Our children therefore commonly end up with a diet of electronic interaction rather than the experience of being with their friends.

Box 12

Computers 'Put Workers at Risk of Mental Illness'

'Spending just five hours a day in front of a computer can hugely increase the risk of depression and insomnia, according to new research. One of the biggest investigations into the hazards of computers in the workplace, involving 25,000 people, has concluded that too much screen time is damaging the mental health of employees ...

Researchers are calling for employees to restrict time spent at terminals after studying the effects on health over a three-year period. "This research suggests the prevention of mental disorders and sleep disorders requires the restriction of computer use to less that five hours a day", said the lead researcher Dr Tetsuya Nakazawa, of Chiba University in Japan.

The results, published in the American Journal of Industrial Medicine, showed that ... once office workers crossed the threshold [of five hours or more a day], the dangers of psychological disorders increased ... Professor Cary Cooper, of the University of Manchester Institute of Science and Technology, said concern was growing over mental health problems caused by working with computers.'

Daily Telegraph, 31 December 2002

Living Together – Separately ...

Robert D. Puttnam has researched into the trend toward greater social isolation and withdrawal from community life. He believes that television has eroded social life, relationships, and trust so that we are increasingly 'bowling alone'. Newspaper-reading, on the other hand, is linked with social engagement. He suggests that TV destroys social capital by time displacement, and by the 'mean and lean world' effect – so heavy TV viewers are unusually cynical about other people, and prone to passivity and pessimism about human nature. The electronic media consume as much time as other discretionary activities such as play, hobbies, sports, visiting friends, and just 'hanging out'. He also suggests that TV is associated with increased aggressiveness though possibly not real violence, and it also undermines schooling. The danger of the electronic media is that it is privatizing our family and community life.[2]

Electronic addiction: the plug-in drug

The electronically triggered withdrawal from social life has also been observed in the work-place. One company found that people were spending up to three hours a day on e-mail – often e-mailing their work 'neighbours' rather than checking in with them personally! One explanation of this withdrawal is that the CRT is a plug-in drug, and that there is a growing incidence of TV dependence. Many people are so hooked that they demonstrate five commonly recognized dependence indicators. These include:

- Many viewers intend to watch one programme, but then watch hour after hour.
- People who accept that they watch too much cannot cut down their viewing.
- Important social activities are sacrificed in favour of viewing.
- The longer you view, the harder it is to switch off.
- Withdrawal symptoms set in after viewing, or when heavy viewers cut back or try stopping altogether.[3]

This is not surprising as the content of TV programmes is carefully crafted to capture attention, and the medium itself *demands* attention. We've all surely had the experience of trying to have a conversation in a room whilst our eyes are being drawn to a TV set!

In sum, television is a powerful medium which adults, let alone children, find it hard to resist. As already discussed, one's eyes are glued to the tube by the fast electronic pace, by a wealth of images, and a multitude of technical events. Highlighted content is designed by programme-makers to hold your attention. The TV/ Brain hypothesis (discussed in Chapter 4) suggests that the CRT 'tunes out' the critical left brain, putting us into a 'spaced-out' state which is open to whatever goes in. As we have already seen, the Emerys consider that radiant, fluorescent TV light 'closes down' the conscious brain and knocks out the decision-making functions that enable one to switch off. To 'view consciously' and critically, one has to resist the basic electrical response of the brain to the TV medium, which is to tune out.

Television addiction is no mere metaphor, according to Robert Kubey and Mihaly Csikszentmihalyi writing in the prestigious *Scientific American* journal.[4] Quoting surveys showing that 10 per cent of adults label themselves as TV addicts, and that seven out of ten teenagers say they spend too much time viewing, they comment that whilst people choose to watch, why is it that so many express misgivings about how much they watch? They posed the key question, 'How does TV addiction happen?'

First, on testing viewers with electroencephalograms (EEGs), they were surprised to discover that viewers' sense of relaxation ended when the set was switched off, but that feelings of passivity and dullness continued. Viewers felt that TV had drained them of energy; they found it harder to concentrate after viewing; and their moods were the same or worse than before. This finding was in stark contrast to reading, hobbies, or sports, after which they felt better.

Yet within moments of switching back on, viewers felt more relaxed again. The researchers concluded that viewers therefore tended to associate viewing with rest and lack of tension – which belief tends to be reinforced when the set is turned off and the tension returns. As with other addictions, TV-viewing results in more viewing – hence the fact that people watch more than they intend to, even though they know that the longer they watch, the less satisfaction they derive from it.

The researchers then asked why TV has such a hold on its viewers. One cause is the fight/ flight or *orienting response* to danger, such as a novel stimulus. Orienting reactions include slowing of the heart, blocking of Alpha waves, constriction of the blood vessels to the muscles, and adrenalin rush. Orienting reactions are triggered by highlighted content, loud noises and technical TV 'events' such as cuts or zooms, thus grabbing the viewers' attention. Hence, people say that 'If the TV is on, I am unable to keep my eyes off it … I feel hypnotized by the screen'. Advertisements in which there are many cuts, commonly at the rate of one or more a second, continuously trigger the orienting response.

The orienting response is deeply rooted, and starts with even 6-week-old babies, who have been observed to attend to a TV's sound and light. Older babies crane their necks, sometimes by as much as 180 degrees, to catch a glimpse.

The most convincing argument that TV addiction is no mere metaphor is that when people cut back on TV, they experience *withdrawal symptoms.* 'The family walked around like a chicken without a head, screamed constantly. Children bothered me, and my nerves were on edge. Tried to interest them in games, but impossible. TV is a part of them.' Where families have been paid to stop viewing for a week or a month, as in the annual *TV-Turnoff Week*, many families experienced conflicts and were unable to finish the experiment.

The extent to which heavy users of the computer and video games are subject to similar levels of dependence is also a matter of considerable concern. There are many children and teenagers who seemed addicted to video games, finding it difficult to walk away from them. Boys seem far more susceptible than girls – for example, to joystick digit, Sega thumb, mouse elbow and, hand/arm vibration syndrome. Vibration white finger was reported by the doctor of a 15-year-old Liverpool boy, who had been playing up to seven hours a day on his Sony Playstation. (Sony puts warnings with its games, advising a 15-minute break every hour, and warning against possible epileptic seizures.)[5]

Whilst computer games offer huge challenges and entertainment, the extended activation of the orienting, fight/flight response can leave players worn out, dizzy, tired, and nauseous. One extreme example of such effects occurred in Japan in 1997, when hundreds of children went to hospital suffering from 'optically stimulated epileptic seizures' triggered by flashing lights from a Pokemon video game seen on television. Parents find that rapid screen movement can cause motion sickness in their children after only 15 minutes. However, many children may continue to play, especially if they are unsupervised or lack self-control.

Box 13

Is the Video Game One of the Most Addictive Products Ever Invented?

When you buy a computer game at £30–45 for your child, you get a potentially addictive activity which may occupy your child for hundreds of hours. Most games are designed to glue players to the action, to reward the player to keep going, to challenge, to engage – and at the end of the game to go back to the beginning, attempt a new level of skill – or buy the next video game. Types of game include the following:

1. Sport simulations – ice hockey, golf, or athletics, e.g. Hole in One.

2. Super Racers, which simulate motor sports, like F1 Race.
3. Adventures, in which players can enter a fantasy world and take on new identities, such as the Addams family.
4. Puzzlers – brainteasers, chess, draughts, etc.
5. Weird or miscellaneous games, such as Sim City – an extended simulation of family and community life.
6. Platform games: these games involve running and jumping on to platforms, like Super Mario Brothers, Skateboards.
7. Platform blasters – also platforms, but involve blasting everything that comes into sight, such as Robocop, Batman.
8. Beat-'em-ups: games that involve physical violence such as punching and kicking, e.g. Street Fighter, Rival Turf.
9. Shot-'em-ups: shooting and killing games using various weapons.

Clearly, computer games are a useful educational and entertainment resource when used carefully – and discerning parents will exercise care in game choice, and rules for the amount of time spent playing. For example, many children will just keep playing unless their parents set limits – and they need help with learning to stop. Some children, if left to themselves, may well become 'keyboard junkies'. You can try assessing computer games players against the five dependence indicators on page 96 to assess whether or not they are addicts.

Professor Mark Griffiths writes, ' … Excessive computer game playing can have potentially damaging effects upon a minority of individuals who display compulsive and addictive behaviour, and who will do anything possible to "feed their addiction". Such individuals need monitoring.' (Mark Griffiths, 'Are computer games bad for children?', *The Psychologist*, September 1993.)

Undermining Play and Childhood

A young child's work is her play. Play involves imitation, re-creation, invention, creativity, and imagination. Through play, a young child first imitates his everyday happenings and then re-creates them dramatically. Play is the gateway to the imagination, but also to acquiring social skills, co-ordination, and an understanding of the world. 'Let's play!' is an invitation to be active, to explore, to have fun, and to imagine. Imaginative play is absorbing and engaging, providing 'soul nourishment' for the rest of life.

Yet according to play researcher Sally Jenkinson, the playful spirit of childhood is under threat. 'Our polarized society – in which we either work or are being entertained – has lost its playfulness.' She describes today's recipe for childhood as being about containment – keeping children occupied, for example by the electronic media, and by the relentless pressures for children to be 'educated' at ever earlier ages. For Jenkinson, 'The cost of accelerating childhood, of "too much too soon", may be a precocious and precarious entry into adulthood – and eventual overload. We may come to realize that a play-deficient child is a disadvantaged child.'[6]

Moreover, there has arguably been an uncritical embracing of PC technology by the schooling system, and some schools can actually increase and compound this disadvantage. Thus, for example, one mother was told by a teacher to provide her 7-year-old son with Nintendo computer games, a Disney Game boy for hand-held computer games, and Pokemon videos to help him catch up with his classmates.

Other factors undermining play include limited play space – for example, no local outdoor play facilities, no playmates, toys that are so 'perfect' or highly finished that they leave nothing to the imagination, and little parental encouragement. Television and computers can steal time away from young children's play; and the grave consequence can be play-deprived children.

'All Jim can use sticks for is guns! He can't imagine them being brooms, spades, spoons, wands, or feathers like the non-television children', a nursery teacher called John commented to me. He continued,

'There were three children playing with a chest of wooden blocks. One (not a viewer) was thoroughly absorbed – it was amazing what came out of him! You could see the difference between him, and another boy of 5 with a high exposure to television. He borrowed ideas and found it hard to play with much inventiveness.'

In the nursery schools and Kindergartens where teachers carefully observe new children's ability to play, John's findings were confirmed, i.e. that heavy viewers are less imaginative and less dramatic in their play, show less initiative, are more likely to expect to be entertained, can pay less attention to stories, sometimes lack co-ordination, and do not play so constructively as light or non-viewing children.

Play researchers distinguish between media-influenced *imitative play* when actions are copied and repeated, and *symbolic play*, where there is imagination, problem-solving, and transformation. In symbolic play, children do the scripting, acting, and directing, working things out in their known way rather than just repeating media content. When in the early 1990s, for example, the TV show, Teenage Mutant Ninja Turtles (TMNT) came out, Kindergarten teachers observed that:

'The play is without any real content. The children only name the characters, and appear to have no notion of what to do except run, threaten, tackle.'

'There is a lack of scripting and little of the involved pretend play children should be doing.'

'The play is all boys and very stereotyped. Boys act strong, macho, violent.'[7]

Children use play to transform their experience into something that is personally meaningful. They work out their own insights as they actively control what they are playing, and it's different for each child. However, teachers observations of TMNT-influenced play was that children were imitating in very similar ways, rather than *really* playing. And when children keep carrying out the same repetitive actions, without any free elaboration or variation, they are stuck – trying to work through media content, but not being able to go beyond it.[8]

Creativity and imagination

Tannis Macbeth Williams found that in Notel (a Canadian mountain town which previously had no television), the introduction of television negatively affected the performance of adults in creative problem-solving tasks. The tasks required thinking of less likely alternatives to the problem, and not getting bogged down in the 'obvious' approaches. The conclusions were that television may lead to 'decreased attention and a lower tolerance of frustration'. The displacement of problem-solving experiences by viewing may result in a more limited repertoire of divergent solutions.[9]

What, however, are the effects of viewing on young children's creativity and imagination? In a paper on toys, Tim Hicks was concerned that the fresh, lively, imaginative receptivity of children is being exploited by the television medium. He writes:

'With television, the manufacturers had direct access to the image-receptive consciousness of children. Children are by nature ready for, needing and unconsciously seeking the images that teach them what the world is and who they are. They look out to discover the world and everything that comes to them adds to their ongoing definition. Being thus growing and forming themselves and their understanding of the world, they are deeply vulnerable to the influence of the images presented on television and become captured by the images. Television is such a powerful manipulating and influencing factor because it places images directly into the consciousness of the child in an almost surgical fashion with the child having almost no barriers with which to protect him- or herself.'[10]

Our children's imaginations are also co-opted and colonized by the penetrating images of the toy manufacturers. Children lose the internal space to create their own images, and they begin to be able to envision and structure their own emerging experience only in the images delivered so persistently by the mass marketers.

Television has thus initiated a process that leads to the stunting of the imagination; and instead of developing one's own imaginative powers as a child, one will merely develop the ability to manipulate images on the screen. Video graphics, for example, enable children to make images on the television screen. One advertisement read: 'Nothing is as mesmerizing to kids as television. Nothing commands so much of their attention or occupies so much of their time … In the beginning it [i.e. TV] controlled them.'

The inability of children to create original images or to play imaginatively can, then, be a direct consequence of media overload in early childhood. Jane Healy, an educational psychologist, observed that,

'Teachers find that today's video immersed children can't form original pictures in their mind or develop imaginative representations. Teachers of young children lament the fact that many now have to be taught to play symbolically or pretend – previously only a symptom of mentally or emotionally disordered youngsters.'[11]

104

Turning Children into Consumers

There are three broad reasons why the electronic media are well designed to 'deliver' children's minds early in their lives for commercial exploitation. Firstly, as we have seen in Chapter 4, the CRT (VDT) 'tunes out' the brain, thus enabling the transmission of images without conscious choice – the ideal advertising medium from the advertiser's point of view.

Secondly, children under 8 years of age are developmentally unable to understand the aims of advertising, tending to accept the claims as true. For this reason, the American Academy of Pediatrics has concluded that all advertising aimed at children is 'inherently deceptive and exploits children under 8 years of age'. The Academy has unsurprisingly declared war on child advertisements: they want to protect children from the 'Gimmes', the advertiser-induced disease of children asking for products advertised on the electronic media.

Since many children see over *20,000* commercials a year, doctors believe that this is seriously influencing the emotional well-being of children. Academy president Saul J. Robinson said that the commercial exploitation of children by means of excessive, inappropriate advertising should cease. Moreover, such commercials were unfair, since young children lacked the requisite critical faculties to evaluate them. Thus, for example, over-8's could more easily see that a commercial was a commercial; and some research found that 5 year olds described commercials as 'showing you things to buy', but that over-8's could see that, 'They're trying to sell you things'.[12, 13]

Thirdly, sophisticated advertising is interwoven with many TV programmes via such techniques as product placement, and with Internet services, so that there is a constant environment of commercial messages. These are integrated into a total marketing strategy through films, videos, toys, food, stories, magazines, clothes, and logos exploiting sophisticated psychological techniques.

As a result, parents are pestered by their children for whatever products are currently being pushed. Advertisers who push the 'pester-power' button are very clear (and, some might say, *cynical*) about their objectives – for children constitute a big market. Advertiser James McNeal frankly acknowledges the great advantage of the vast children's market:

'Children under the age of eight believe advertising unconditionally, tend to see it as a logical part of programming, and tend not to see the selling intent of it. Advertising to children is virtually all emotion and persuasion. Advertisers put to work all the creativity they can muster to create a fantasy environment, with very little regard to useful information expressed in ways children can understand. Advertisers have the ability to convince children to like and desire practically any product, yet this ability is applied mainly to toys and sugared foods.'[14]

However, he goes on brazenly to advocate that 'Children should be viewed as super special consumers deserving of super special treatment by the marketing system. This is necessary only for a short time, while the children are becoming fully qualified consumers, and it will guarantee happier and more effective customers for all marketeers for all time.'

The advertisers have therefore proactively *created* the teenage, teenybopper, weenie-bopper, tween, and now even the infant market. Companies selling sweets, ice cream, music, books, records, clothes, and toys depend on the child market, and they do everything they deem necessary to encourage and maintain a continuous flow of child consumers. Since children imitate what they see, and since television has the power to influence our language, minds, perception of reality, and the fabric of our consciousness, then *such commercial exploitation constitutes a massive intervention into young children's lives.*

But even though children's ability to detect the selling intent of advertisements improves with age, should not all children have the right to be free from advertising? – and parents the right to be free of pester power? One simple way is to legislate against all TV and Internet advertising aimed at children, as has already occurred in Quebec and in Sweden. Such a ban would result in a quieter childhood, freer of commercial exploitation, with more space to play, enabling children to think for themselves and develop their own imaginations and values.

Box 14

Approaches to Countering 'Pester Power'

1. Be as clear and as firm as possible about what children can or cannot have; and keep to agreements. The more parents can experience and convey a firm inner authority and conviction in their very being (which is crucially different from simply being authoritarian), the less likely it is that children will continue to pester.
2. Be clear about decisions – 'I have decided not to buy this'. Explain decisions if appropriate, e.g. 'I cannot afford this'.
3. Plan and discuss in advance what you will buy when shopping; children are then less influenced by displays, and more focused on what you have agreed.
4. Saying 'no' is OK – it helps children get used to limits.
5. Give regular pocket money, and encourage saving for valued things.
6. Encourage children to value people for who they are, rather than for their possessions.
7. Lobby your political representatives (MPs, MEPs, government ministers, local councillors) to back campaigns to stop advertising directed at children.

Anti-social Behaviour and Violence

The debate about the effects of the electronic media on children's behaviour is still going on. Some people, like Lt Col. Dave Grossman, maintain that video games and media violence are teaching children to kill, thus affording a plausible explanation for the multiple shootings at Columbine School in Colorado or Erfurt in Germany. Child psychologist Urie Bronfenbenner thinks that the socialization of children stops when the TV is turned on, 'So when you turn on TV, you turn off the process of making human beings human.' Researchers Jerome and Dorothy Singer of Yale University concluded that,

' … heavy television viewing puts children at risk of increased aggression and restlessness with all the negative cognitive and social consequences of such a behaviour pattern. Those of us who have been active over more than 15 years in studying a variety of aspects of the television medium in a reasonably scientific fashion cannot fail to be impressed with significance of this medium for the emerging consciousness of the developing child.' [15]

They argue that protecting children against media violence is therefore of great importance.

Others maintain that media violence does not result in more aggression and anti-social behaviour amongst children. When, for example, TV was introduced to the island of St Helena in the early 1990s, children did not show signs of increased aggression. It is also said that media violence can be positive – offering ways to trans-form aggression, just as some violent children's stories can assist in working through life problems.

The debate will no doubt continue, though ordinary people note the intriguing contradiction between the claims of TV advertisers that they significantly change people's buying behaviour on the one hand, and on the other, claims by media pundits that the heavy viewing by children of violent programme content is harmless.

Something that researchers are agreed upon, however, is that heavy viewers tend to perceive the world to be meaner and leaner than do light viewers. Heavy viewers consistently overestimated the likelihood of encountering violence as opposed to light viewers, who had a much more accurate perception. The more violence seen on the media, the more threatened, anxious, and defensive people felt – to the point of having burglar alarms, protective walls, and guard dogs.

Another consideration is the high levels of aggressive and violent behaviour shown by the electronic media. There are various estimates that children can see, on average, up to 8,000 murders by the end of primary school, and over 16,000 by the age of 18, together with an astounding 200,000 violent acts.[16] With access to the Internet and video, moreover, some children may be exposed to far more violence.

As argued earlier, young children find it hard to distinguish reality from what they view, so violent TV scenes are of course very real to them. Even infants of 14 months have been seen to imitate violent cartoon and slapstick violence.[17] When aggressive or violent behaviour is learnt at a young age, it is hard to unlearn: for example, a 22-year longitudinal study concluded that 'violent television watched in childhood correlated positively with subsequent behaviour as an adult'.[18]

So how does viewing affect children's behaviour? One naturalistic experiment was carried out in the Canadian Rockies by Tannis Macbeth Williams, on how TV came to the town of Notel. She found that the aggressive behaviour of Notel children increased significantly following the introduction of television. The effects showed up in both girls and boys, and for both verbal and physical aggression. Children initially low in aggression showed increases, and not just the children who were initially high in aggression.

These effects were so marked as to be observed two years after television came to Notel. The results could not be explained by IQ differences or put down to social class. TV-viewing in general, rather than specific programmes, seemed to be the cause.[19] Psychological processes of imitation, desensitization, and disinhibition can explain the increase in aggressive behaviour.

Imitation

Just as children may learn positive behaviour from television – such as a child saving the life of another child from suffocation by dislodging a bone, having seen the method demonstrated on television – so behaviour can be learnt from negative role models too. As already discussed, young children learn through imitating other people, and the 'role models' they copy are very important for social learning. It follows that the imitation of aggressive role models through media learning can increase children's verbal and physical aggression. Sporadic attention to violent highlights, and the lack of understanding by young children of the links between aggressive actions and punishments, may be several of the mechanisms involved. Children, especially if there are no positive alternatives shown, nor any sanctions, will copy scenes of aggressive interaction when they are shown many times over.

W.A. Belson proved that children imitate toughs in an exhaustive scientific study of a sample of 1,565 London boys in 1972–3, who were interviewed about their viewing habits and attitudes to violence. Dr Belson found that, even taking into account over 227 variables such as size, physical strength, family size, neighbourhood, or divorce in the family, television violence had an effect over and above these factors. He concluded that 'The evidence is strongly supportive of the hypothesis that long-term exposure to television violence increases the degree to which boys engage in serious violence.'[20]

Immunization, desensitization, and disinhibition

As well as the imitation of and identification with aggressive role models, media violence may immunize and desensitize children. Violence occurs when physical or mental injury, hurt, or death is inflicted on people. By viewing violence regularly, one can become immunized against violence and horror. As a result, it may be accepted as a natural part of life. Children repeatedly exposed to violence on television were less likely to respond positively to victims of real-life violence.

Desensitization is a process that whittles away normal feelings in people, until they can be relaxed and at ease whilst watching events that would have otherwise aroused the gravest concern. The thousands of killings, the murders, fights and other violent incidents shown on television may be aptly described as mass desensitization.

Another factor is that *television removes inhibitions* in people that would otherwise prevent them from behaving violently. Through disinhibition, people no longer feel hampered by 'conscience', feelings of guilt, shame, or embarrassment. One of the famous social psychologist Stanley Milgram's experiments was set up to demonstrate the disinhibiting effect of a violent film. Subjects were asked to administer 'electric shocks' to another person when they made a mistake. In fact, the victim only pretended to suffer. Of two groups, the members of the first who had seen a knife fight from the film 'Rebel Without a Cause' punished mistakes far more severely than those in the second group who had only seen a harmless education film. When violent methods of solving problems in everyday life are frequently shown on the media, the result may well be disinhibition.

Stereotyping

Another form of violence is the portrayal of groups of people in stereotyped ways – for example, gender role stereotyping, ageism, and racism. Stereotyping causes people to be violent to others because the process undermines the ability to see and relate to people as individuals.

In the town of Notel, Williams found that children's ' ... sex-role attitudes, that is, beliefs about appropriate and typical behaviour for girls and boys, were more strongly sex-typed in the presence than in the absence of television'.[21]

Box 15

Dummying Down!

'Throughout all the hours of children's programmes I watched, one message was utterly consistent: men and boys are stupid and contemptible. Furthermore, they are technically inept, emotionally clueless, and – although obsessed with girls – sexually inadequate ...

At present, BBC children's television is fixated upon S Club 7: they feature in a drama series (set in the U.S.) and then they turn up repeatedly on other shows. Without exception the girls in these groups are promoted as smart, aggressive and domineering. The boys sing in high, breathy soprano voices and serve as the butt of jokes.

Last Saturday morning, BBC1 screened a scene in which these young women ... were talking in a kitchen. When one of them expressed nervousness about getting her man, another showed her what to do: she shoved the nearest boy up against the fridge, grabbed his head in both hands, shoved her tongue down his throat, stepped back, slapped him, and knocked him over ...'
Christopher Dunkley, 'Dummying down!' (a TV critic spends a week watching children's programmes), *Daily Mail*, 23 November 2002, pp. 30–1

To conclude, it seems clear that the processes of stereotyping, observational learning, imitation, identification, immunization, desensitization, physical arousal, disinhibition, and justification (i.e. the violence of TV heroes justifies the aggression of viewers) can cause increased anti-social behaviour.

Fortunately, parents and teachers work hard to socialize children, thus countering as far as they are able the negative effects of the electronic media, whilst building on the positives. For example, when TV was introduced into the isolated South Atlantic island of St Helena in the early 1990s, there were already such positive social norms that the side-effects of TV made little impact. School playground videos, for example, showed very high levels of care taken by children of each other, and low levels of bullying; and this sociable behaviour continued after the introduction of television.[22]

However, mainstream societies are very different from the supportive community culture of St Helena. Lt Col. Dave Grossman, formerly an army ranger, a psychology lecturer at West Point, and advisor on post-traumatic shock to emergency health and police teams, believes that video game violence is training children to kill. His arguments are a stark wake-up call, even though some academics do argue that the casual relationship between rising levels of social violence and the spread of the electronic media may be neither clear-cut nor straightforward.

Grossman starts by asking, 'Where does a 14 year old boy who never fired a gun before get the skill and the will to kill?' He uses the example of Michael Carneal, who stole a .22 pistol and shot eight students at a Paducah (Kentucky) high-school prayer group, hitting eight children with eight shots. Hardened soldiers were stunned by this 'achievement', by how this boy learned to kill better than trained professionals. In a similar case, on 26th April 2002, Robert Steinhauser shot 13 of his teachers at Gutenburg Gymnasium, Erfurt, Germany.

According to Grossman, there has been a worldwide increase of violence since the 1950s, though this has been masked in the West by the fact that the murder rate has been restricted by better life-saving methods. The aggravated assault rate of attempted murder has gone up from 60 per 100,000 in 1957 to over 440 per 100,000 by the mid 1990s – an increase of over seven times. After looking at possible causes, Grossman identifies the common factor of *media violence being presented as entertainment for children.*

As a military psychologist, Grossman was asked by the US Army to help train soldiers to kill, which he did by means of removing inhibitions, by brutalizing men in boot camps, by conditioning and rewards, by training knee-jerk reactions, by repetition, desensitization, and by role modelling. But he found that children were being trained to kill as well – but without the safeguards. The American Academy of Pediatrics Task Force on Juvenile Violence found that 'Children are learning to kill from abuse and violence in the home, and most pervasively, from violence as entertainment in television, the movies, and interactive video games.'[23]

If children from 18 months of age are exposed to media violence, they will imitate this, whilst they are still not able to distinguish fact from virtual reality, as discussed earlier. So when young children see media violence, *it is as though it were actually happening.* Inevitably, some children – especially when there are intersecting and reinforcing family environments – will be more prone to accepting such violence as a survival skill in a mean world, like being brutalized in a boot camp.

Grossman cites the 1992 *Journal of the American Medical Association (JAMA)*, which researched into the impact of TV violence. Brandon Centerwell was an epidemiologist who researched murder rates for the Atlanta Center for Disease Control. After controlling methodologically for such factors as economic growth, social unrest, age, alcohol use, and the availability of guns, he concluded that murder rates doubled as a result of the introduction of TV.[24]

When television first appears, there is an immediate explosion of violence on the playground, and after 15 years, the murder rate doubles. This is how long it takes for the proportion of brutalized 2 year olds to get to the 'prime crime' years. The *JAMA* reported that

> 'The introduction of television in the 1950s caused a subsequent doubling of the homicide rate, i.e. long-term childhood exposure to television is a causal factor behind approximately one-half of the homicides committed in the US, or approximately 10,000 homicides annually ... [I]f, hypothetically, television technology had never been developed, there would today be 10,000 fewer homicides each year in the US, 70,000 fewer rapes, and 700,000 fewer injurious assaults.'[25]

Centerwell and Grossman maintain that the electronic media have actually shifted our violence threshold, immunizing many people to violence, so that the extreme element that may commit violent acts commit more of them. And highly relevant to this book's concerns, Centerwall argues that one way to stop what he calls this 'epidemic of violence' is *to take TV sets out of children's bedrooms.*[26]

According to Grossman, then, the evidence for linking the media with rising levels of violence in society is stronger than the link between lung cancer and smoking. His arguments were supported by a research article in the January 2002 issue of *Science* magazine.[27] Grossman points to a key conclusion of the research – viz. that 'The recent *Science* magazine article made it clear that viewing anything over one hour per day can have a profoundly negative effect on long-term behavior.'[28]

Other military methods for disinhibiting killing are classical conditioning, for example through the rewarding of 'correct' behaviour; and operant conditioning, involving stimulus/response learning – for example, as when a child plays an interactive point-and-shoot video game. Lastly, just as in the military, soldiers emulate role models, so the media provide violent role models for children and teenagers to copy and aspire to. This is one reason why the pictures of juvenile killers are not now put on television, lest these trigger copycat, cluster killings. When CBS President Leslie Moonves was asked if he believed that the school massacre at Littleton, Colorado was linked with the media, he said, 'Anyone who thinks the media has nothing to do with it is an idiot.'

Robert Steinhauser, the Gutenburg School killer, was heavily influenced by violent video games that were banned in Germany. At 19, he was expelled from school for forging absence forms. His parents were not informed – they thought he was still studying for his final exams. He had few friends, and was quiet and withdrawn. He built up a virtual world in his bedroom, where the police found sound tracks of bands like the Slipknots' 'Life is Shit', and violent computer games that enabled the player to practise deliberate and cold-blooded killing. Robert learned how to shoot with real guns at the local gun club led by a police superintendent.

On the day of the school murders, 2,000 Erfurt computer fans were going to play a virtual killing game called *Counter-Strike* – but in the event it was called off. Such games were originally developed by the military as simulation games to train soldiers in reflex killing. Hence the $130 million Paducah, Kentucky law suit against the video game company, that claims a link between the violent game and Michael Carneal's murders.[29]

Chapter 7 continues with an examination of the cognitive and learning impacts upon children of a pervasive screen culture.

In a Nutshell ...

1. The 'mean and lean' view of the world conveyed by the media has encouraged a bedroom screen culture in homes, with what Dr Sonia Livingstone calls 'a lot of scared parents and a lot of trapped kids'.

2. According to the *Scientific American,* the electronic media are addictive, both from the tuning-out effect of the CRT, and the fast-paced content which grabs attention through activating the 'orienting response'. Impressionable children need faithful protection from the plug-in drug from an early age, as with other drugs such as alcohol or tobacco.

3. The electronic media can undermine creativity, play, the imagination, problem-solving, social skills, and literacy.

4. The electronic media are well designed for turning children into consumers and for commercializing childhood. Research indicates that children under 8 find it difficult if not impossible to discern the selling messages in advertisements. The American Academy of Pediatrics therefore concludes that advertising aimed at children is 'inherently deceptive and exploits children under 8 years of age'.

5. The evidence for linking the electronic media with rising levels of social violence is stronger than are the demonstrated causal links between lung cancer and smoking. Virtual killing-games such as *Counter-Strike* have been linked with the disturbed young men responsible for school massacres.

7. Social Hazards II

Cognitive and Learning Effects

Just as the benefits of TV were hyped in the early days, so computers are now being promoted as 'so educationally beneficial'. The assumptions behind this high-tech commercial push into schools are, firstly, that computers greatly improve both teaching and learning, and secondly, that even young children must become computer literate quickly so as to improve their ability to obtain the best jobs in tomorrow's world.

The idea that computers improve learning in schools is based on anecdotes, but according to Edward Miller, a former editor of the *Harvard Education Letter*, the research 'is so flawed it shouldn't even be called research. It's just worthless'.[1] Thus, for example, British Prime Minister Tony Blair wants a computer on every child's desk, so that computers will ultimately oust schoolbooks. One piece of evidence driving this intention was that a literacy computer package was allegedly found to help children of 3 years of age to recognize simple sentences and therefore to read!

Box 16

'Computers in the Classroom Are "a Waste of Millions"'

'Computers in the classroom do not improve pupils' learning, a major study suggests. It found evidence that money lavished on information technology for schools is likely to have been largely wasted. It would have been better spent on more teachers. Researchers studied one of the world's biggest schools computerisation programmes ... In some subjects, particularly maths, computer teaching appears to have slowed the pace of learning. The study, published by the Royal Economic Society [in the Economic Journal], ... was based on the performance of pupils in Israel after the state lottery poured millions into school computerisation in the 1990s ... Professor Angrist, from the Massachusetts Institute of Technology, and Professor Lavy, of the Hebrew University of Jerusalem, said, "This significant and ongoing expenditure on education technology does not appear to be justified by pupil performance results. Money spent on computers would have been better spent on other things." ... The computerisation cost £60 million, enough to pay for four extra teachers for a year in each of the 905 schools involved.'

Steve Doughty, Social Affairs Correspondent, *Daily Mail,*
25 October 2002, p. 29

The second argument, that if children do not acquire IT skills they will not get the best jobs, is at the very least hollow. The rate of change of technology and employment is such that it is difficult, if not impossible to predict what the job market will be like in even just a few years' time. When asked, employers say that the necessary IT skills can be taught in just a few weeks, and often more systematically than in schools. What employers want is young people who are motivated, who can learn and think for themselves, are adaptable and creative, and who have good communication skills and a broad experience of life.

Critics such as Todd Oppenheimer in *The Computer Delusion*, the Alliance for Childhood's important research report *Fool's Gold*, and Alison Armstrong and Charles Casement's *The Child and the Machine* are, to say the least, highly sceptical about the benefits of the electronic media for children's learning, particularly for children under 7 years of age. Oppenheimer points out that the 36-person Clinton Technology Task Force which advocated a computer in every classroom was made up of technology advocates. Two-thirds worked in the media or high-tech industries; and when asked if they had considered any negative effects of computers in schools, they said that there weren't any. The relative merits of other interventions such as smaller class sizes and more teachers, more art, music, literacy, better nutrition, more money spent on books or libraries, or better school buildings were simply not considered.

The risks to children's education and growth from the electronic media include the following:

- the undermining of creativity and intellectual development;
- virtual reality and real experience;
- language and literacy;
- reading;
- poor attention and concentration.

Each of these factors will be considered in turn.

The undermining of creativity and intellectual development

Reading programmes, quite apart from their use of an electronic medium rather than a book and real human contact to teach reading, have received poor reviews. For example, a reading programme called 'Reader Rabbit', used in over 100,000 US schools, resulted in a 50 per cent decline in measures of children's creativity. And when pre-schoolers used the programme for 7 months, they were then unable to answer simple questions, and showed poor skills in creative brainstorming.

Creative work requires children to be original, bring inner pictures alive – to dream and to play. As Albert Einstein said, imagination and experience are the foundations of knowledge – and if you want your child to be intelligent, tell them stories. However, a diet of ready-made images from the electronic media leave little if any space for nurturing the imagination. Children often need the stimulus of open space and free time to develop creativity and resourcefulness. One German play experiment with children tried taking all their toys away from them for a month. After initially being at a loss, the Kindergarten children soon began to play inventively, creating all kinds of resourceful activities with whatever simple everyday objects were around.[2]

Virtual reality and real experience

Children simply love learning from direct experience – experiential learning – with the sense of wonder and exciting discovery that come from experiencing the natural world. Whether it is stargazing, catching frogs, or watching badgers at night, the Internet just cannot compete! Clifford Stoll says that *the real* needs to come before *the virtual*: 'I'd rather read a sixth grader's composition on butterflies written after watching a monarch chrysalis in a field of milkweed than view a multimedia display referencing the latest entomological research downloaded from the Internet.'[3]

Language and literacy

The electronic media can profoundly affect language and literacy. In the research referred to earlier, for example, Dr Sally Ward found that one in five pre-school children suffered delayed language development due to lack of speaking with parents, and the constant noise from stereo and TV (see pages 71–2). In Birmingham, an early-language project was started in a deprived suburb to encourage mothers to talk with their babies and toddlers. Local teachers found that the vocabulary of the children entering nursery school was contracting, and that their speech was limited.

Several causes were suggested for the infants' poor language skills, such as the replacement of terrace housing by high-rise flats, the break-up of large families, the number of single-parent families, isolated children, and parents not playing or speaking so much with babies. However, television was also thought to be a factor, as discovered in Sally Ward's research. Television has also undermined the transmission of nursery rhymes, according to the Assistant Mistresses' Association.[4]

According to infant teachers, nursery rhymes are of vital importance in developing the speech, language, and numeracy of young children. Rhymes like 'One, Two, Three, Four, Five, once I caught a fish alive', or 'Ten Green Bottles', teach numbers, words, and rhymes, and they are also facilitative of improved physical co-ordination. Vocabularies are also widened through rhymes like 'Humpty Dumpty' and 'This is the House that Jack Built'. Children taught such family rhymes may know as many as 2,000 words by the age of 5, and be able to take in colour, shape, and numbers. However, many children had only a vocabulary of 50 words on coming to school, which may be attributed, at least in part, to the effects of television.

The Assistant Mistresses' working party was headed by Mrs Pierce-Price, who described nursery rhymes as 'a foreign art'. According to members of the working party, even though nursery rhymes were found on television, children failed to learn them. They thought that a reason for children not knowing nursery rhymes was because television was a 'look and forget' rather than a 'look and *learn*' medium.

Children learn to speak through imitating, listening to, and conversing with real, live people. They need to make contact through other speakers with the 'genius' of language, with its life, sense, and movement. Electronically reproduced voices are simply no substitute for real conversation. The electronic media may blunt a commitment to language by delaying the development of the verbal areas of the brain – at a crucially 'language-sensitive' age or 'developmental window'.

The importance of 'Mum, speak to me' cannot be over-emphasized. Babies first hear conversation around them, and understand a great deal when we converse with them. In the later months they exercise their vocal organs through 'babbling', and begin to imitate words, often repeating them over and over again. The screen, as opposed to a brother, sister, or parent, does not wait for a response, nor does it have a smiling face or a warm hug.

Imitation, rehearsal, and repetition help the toddler to master words, phrases, and meanings from other people – conversation being the optimal condition for language development. Repeating rhymes like 'Little Bo Peep' or 'Pat-a-cake Pate-a-Cake Baker's Man' help with clarity of speech, with securing a real feel for the language, and for discovering the excitement in words and in rhythm. A child with a rich fund of nursery rhymes, songs, and stories will certainly have a head start at school.

One hospital play therapist described the case of a little boy brought in with a 'speech deficiency'. He watched a lot of television, was gun crazy, and had a limited vocabulary. The words he used most frequently were 'Bang! Bang!', and the boy suffered multiple speech difficulties. Therapy and the limiting of his TV-viewing resulted in immediate speech gains.

A key factor for language development at home and at school, therefore, is the extent to which conversation and real human inter-relating occur. The one constant factor that enables children to speak well is supportive talking with more competent speakers, rather than with the electronic media. When children enter school or Kindergarten at 4 or 5 years of age, their language needs to be encouraged so as to build a rich fluency. Face-to-face conversation is therefore the best way of developing language, rather than interactive software. And confident readers were often, first of all, good reciters and speakers.

Reading

When I was visiting a class of 8 year olds at a local school, the teacher pointed out several 'lazy readers'. They could read perfectly well, but were either not interested enough to read, or found it difficult to get 'inside' what they were reading. Such lazy readers found the necessary concentration, focusing of attention, and effort hard to maintain. In addition, the teacher found that their comprehension of what was being read was somewhat vague. Significantly, he linked this with a diet of the electronic media at home, and the lack of a domestic 'reading habit'. Certain non-viewing children in the class read regularly at home, and these latter children did very well in school.

Since the 1980s in Britain, an achievement gap of 16 per cent in literacy has opened up between boys and girls at 11 years of age, and of 10 per cent at 16 years. Teachers are puzzled, and the experts disagree about the causes, whilst popular surveys show that boys are shunning books for TV and computer games – which they find more exciting and interactive than books, which are 'boring'. It could be that the rise of computer games since the late 1980s has been more directed to boys, and that reading is seen as a more female pursuit.

Literacy – reading and writing – is basic to our society. People who are illiterate feel themselves to be outsiders or even stigmatized. Writing and reading are therefore vital skills, though one can sometimes feel a trace old-fashioned in having to 'stick up' for literacy in an electronic age.

We now live in an 'electronic age' in which images are displacing printed words. Until the print age, most cultures were oral. When I was doing social research in the Faroes, I encountered a rich oral tradition through the old people there. At festival times, far into the early hours of the morning, they would recite the ancient sagas, myths, stories, and ballads of their people. In former days, children in such cultures entered the imaginative world through listening, learning, and reciting the old sagas and stories.

The relics of the oral tradition still survived for young children into the print age. Stories were told to children before bedtime, nursery rhymes and games were learnt by children who explored the world of imagination, of language, poetry, and music through adults. Teachers saw the cultivation of such a rich oral culture for children as a sound pre-school preparation for literacy. Indeed, in middle European Kindergarten education, such as in the global Steiner (Waldorf) school movement, the aim was to develop rich play, and social and language skills as a preparation for school proper at around 7 years of age.

Now, however, the electronic media are having a very strong influence on the pre-school culture of children – whether it's a bedtime video or computer games. The reading of books has now sadly been displaced as school-age children's number one leisure pursuit.

Many people feel in their hearts that reading is 'better' than viewing for children. Comparing the nature of the two media is instructive. Reading needs concentration, focusing, thought, imagination, and the ability to have 'inner vision', to visualize. Television requires little concentration, de-focuses the mind, lames the capacity for visualization by the substitution of electronically produced images, and encourages passive brains (see Chapter 4). A reader can vary the pace, or even put down a book if it becomes too exciting, whereas the CRT screen controls the pace and forces the brain to pay attention, making it difficult for children to switch off, as discussed earlier. The reader is in charge of the book, but the television or video game is usually in control of the viewer. Reading a book allows one to create one's own unique pictures of events and people, at one's own pace, and encourages understanding. Television conveys the same interpretation of a novel, such as *The Secret Garden*, to millions of viewers. Each person reading a book creates their own version. Furthermore, whilst children who read can also write, and hence understand the medium they are using, it does not take any skills to watch.

Research into brain-wave patterns backs up the differences mentioned above between television and print. Testing the electrical responses of the brain to print and television gave 'a picture of relaxed attention, interest, and mental activity' in response to reading. The television response was a relaxed drowsy condition with signs of boredom. There were a lot of alpha waves – people who watch television may tend to fall into alpha as if staring at a blank visual field.

This research was confirmed by psycho-physiologist Thomas Mulholland, and Peter Crown, a professor of television and psychology at Hampshire College, Massachusetts, who connected electrodes to the heads of both adult and child viewers. The researchers believed beforehand that children who were viewing exciting programmes would show patterns of high attention. In other words, they would react to the content of the show. They were very surprised when the results showed precisely the reverse. Viewers showed greatly increased alpha waves, indicating passivity, as if they were 'just sitting quietly in the dark'.[5]

To summarize: when reading, one is attentive, aware of one's awareness, in control of the pace of the book, and actively engaged in re-creating the story. When viewing, one is distracted, barely conscious, under the control of the television, and passively receiving images in an automatic way. Not only is the implication of Mulholland's work that television is a training course in inattention, but that whilst viewing, the self, one's 'I', is barely present as an active centre of one's thoughts, feelings, and actions. One is 'spaced out' of one's mind, and one's conscious self is temporarily absent, leaving the television to imprint its images subconsciously on an open mind and organism.

Television-viewing is therefore a totally different experience from reading: television trains short attention spans, while reading stimulates long attention spans; and books are written to keep children's attention – not to grab it and constantly interrupt it. TV is full of images and fast-paced action; reading involves thinking, reflection, and moving at one's own pace. One can put a book down, and pick it up again.

Young children usually look at books, with adults or older children who read to them. Books are *a social experience* – you can talk about them and share them at bedtime. Television for young children is often an *anti-social* experience – with limited conversation, perhaps alone and just watching. Television also gives answers all the time – whereas children learn most effectively by asking questions.

Since many parents ask me during discussions about when it is appropriate for children to start viewing, I often suggest the time *after* they have learned to enjoy reading. Until the reading habit has been firmly established, at from 7 to 9 years of age, viewing may undermine reading skills and enjoyment. One research finding that backs this up was that Jerome and Dorothy Singer of Yale University found that light viewers learned to read more easily than heavy viewers.

Tannis Macbeth William's study of Notel, Canada found that second graders (8 year olds) scored higher on a test of reading fluency than did the second graders in Unitel or Multitel where there was television. Four years later, when TV was available in Notel, there was no difference amongst second graders with regard to reading fluency. Williams argued that one explanation was that TV-viewing holds up the ability to read by using time that would otherwise be spent with books.

Poor attention and concentration

The rise of various kinds of attention problems amongst children since the early 1950s has been linked partly with factors such as sedentary lifestyles, noisy homes that cause children to switch off, junk foods, lack of attention by adults, and the constant background of the electronic media from an early age.

School success requires children to concentrate, focus, listen, remember, and persevere with activities for a reasonable length of time. It follows that children who find it hard to pay attention find school difficult, and can react by becoming disruptive. One cause of attention deficit and hyperactivity is children's pursuit of constant stimulation in a restless, chronic way. When such children enter a much slower-paced school environment, they experience a lack of stimulation, and suffer withdrawal symptoms. Over-exposure to a rapid-fire electronic world during early childhood development leads to sensory addiction which the slower-paced school setting cannot satisfy.

Interestingly, families with haphazard daily life rhythms, and hurried parenting and heavy viewing, have been identified as being implicated in attention disorders. Children relied more heavily on the electronic media, watching more than their peers; and children of heavy-viewing parents are more likely to have attention-deficit difficulties.[6]

Although there may be a small percentage of children where such attention problems are genuinely physiological, an all-too-easy response for over a million American children has been the drug Ritalin, which does calm children down, though with decidedly unhealthy side-effects. Child psychologist John Rosemond also thinks that the electronic media are like 'speed for children'. 'Ritalin may work temporarily, but pharmaceutical intervention won't change behavioural and motivational problems.' After all, children with attention-deficit problems 'can only sit still for shows on television'. Rosemond began by asking what in his home could be influencing his son's attention-deficit symptoms. When they got rid of their TV set, he observed his son's behaviour improve within 6 weeks. Perhaps predictably, however, Rosemond's simple, medication-free solution got him into trouble with parents who felt that their own family lifestyles would be threatened without recourse to Ritalin.[7]

So instead of addressing a major cause of attention difficulties in the form of over-stimulating, fast-paced lifestyles, the problem is fixed with a drug. Children who have been struggling to adapt to an over-stimulating world, who have become addicted to high levels of sensory overload, are then given another drug which may further compound their difficulties.[8]

Schools have been pressurized into adopting more and more information technology and learning software. A computer is now compulsory in British infants school classrooms and in the National Curriculum. However, more exposure to electronic software at schools may simply compound and exacerbate attention disorders, and in the process displacing, for example, the activity of learning to read with a *real* book and a *real* person. The worse thing that teachers or parents can do for hyperactive children is to give them video games or educational software. What they need is a calmer, more structured environment that is engaging and nourishing.

Another effect is that education is influenced in the direction of becoming 'edu-tainment' – fun, with instant gratification. Healthy learning requires challenges, patience, and discipline, making connections through method and application. Jane Healy considers that educational software offers 'electronically sugar coated "learning" that may spoil children's appetite for the main course'.[9] Turning learning into an easy game runs the danger of cheating children out of 'the joy of personal mastery'.[10]

Conclusion: 'Jump-starting' Children with 'Too Much, Too Soon'

Children take their time in growing up, if they are to become healthy, whole adults. A rich childhood lays positive foundations for life. However, if the pace of growth is forced, then 'early ripe, early rot'. A rapid-fire family culture of 'too much too soon' may suit adult agendas and allay short-term anxieties – but it leads to children without a childhood. Children can be very adaptable, of course, but there are limits. One limit is that CRT/VDT technology is fundamentally maladaptive: children's brains simply can't cope with it well, if at all. It is a very powerful, stimulating medium. And as we have seen, the content of programmes and video games is geared to demand attention.

Yet, in spite of the dangers of 'too much, too soon', some parents, and the software industry, are even aiming to jump-start *babies* with computer programs. Jump Start Baby, known as 'Jump Ahead' in Britain, offers point and click games for naming body parts and clothes, and peek-a-boo activities. The image of children here is that they are machines or biocomputers that need 'starting up'. Yet as copious research evidence will testify, such jump-starting can damage children's brains, as we have already seen.

Research by developmental psychologists into child development is constantly coming up with startling new information about how children learn in the early years. Jane Healy, for example, has convincingly argued that the electronic media can be hazardous to young children's brains and learning.[11] Dr Sally Goddard Blythe has convincingly observed how singing and music help children to develop, after noticing how well average students were learning in cathedral-based British choir schools.[12] Such researchers have found how movement can unlock children's learning potential. Sally Jenkinson's research also shows compellingly just how children's resourceful play prepares them for creative imaginative work in adult life.[13]

This research reflects the practice followed in some schools, such as Rudolf Steiner (Waldorf) Kindergartens, where educators aim to help children learn the right thing at the developmentally appropriate time, when they are ready, rather than imposing an uncritical 'too much too soon' ideology. Thus, for example, children up to 7 years of age learn play, movement, social skills, listening, develop language, experience the world through a rich sensory diet, enjoy stories, and engage in simple craft activities such as baking. This lays the foundation for cognitive learning at 7 years and beyond, when children are developmentally ready for formal schooling.

We will conclude with Jane Healy's grave expression of concern at how the electronic media can be hazardous to children's brains and learning – arguments which should surely act as a wake-up call to all educators and educational policy-makers:

'Research strongly indicates that it has the potential to affect both the brain itself and related learning abilities. Abilities to sustain attention independently, stick to problems actively, listen intelligently, read with understanding, and use language effectively may be particularly at risk. No one knows how much exposure is necessary to make a difference. Likewise, no information is available about the overall effects on intelligence of large amounts of time taken from physical exercise, social or independent play, reading, sustained conversation, or roaming quietly about in one's own imagination.'[14]

In a Nutshell ...

1. Children take their time in developing, and developmental psychologists warn against jump-starting childhood with the electronic media. Other activities such as play, music, art, and stories do much more for children's learning and development.

2. Claims about the alleged educational benefits of the electronic media for young children need very careful scrutiny. All too often, there is a notable lack of valid research to support such claims, and also a brazen recourse to fear – 'your children will get behind in the job market if they fail to acquire IT skills at 6 years of age!'

8. Growing up with Screen Culture
When Should Children Start?

The wealth of available research evidence reviewed in earlier chapters, then, points to the compelling conclusion that the electronic media's negative effects on young children substantially outweigh any positive effects. Designed to capture and keep children's attention, the CRT screen is a powerful electronic drug which many adults, let alone young children, find difficult to switch off.

Families are faced today with an ever-faster-paced, electronically geared '24/7' society, which is having a profound influence on the dotcom generation. Millions of children in the USA and Britain are being diagnosed with 'Attention Deficit Hyperactivity Disorder' (ADHD), and the emergence of so-called' 'explosive children' with very low frustration-tolerance levels has recently been observed. More and more adults are suffering stress-related illnesses, with the newly named stress outbursts of desk-, road-, and air rage.

Many of us have hitherto – and understandably – welcomed the new electronic technologies. We responded positively by asking how we might best use them in our work and family environments. Yet given the powerful research evidence on the pervasive and disturbing negative effects of screen culture on children's growth and development, we now face some fundamental questions:

- How can we use the television and the computer constructively in our families, without them taking over and dominating our lives?
- Do we want to calm the pace of our family life by setting limits?
- When is it healthy for our children to start watching – and for how long?

This latter issue sometimes creeps up on parents surreptitiously. The parents of one family got so fed up with their four children's excessive viewing that they threw out the sets, so that they are now a family of avid readers. There were withdrawal symptoms – one child, for example, threatened to sue her parents for cruelty to children!

How, then, can parents make conscious and responsible choices about media use? In my experience as a parent, the most helpful question to ask yourself is, 'How healthy are the electronic media for my child – and for myself?' Then, to help answer this question, observe your child watching TV, playing computer games, or using the computer, and ask yourself if you like what you see. Observe your child playing, drawing, or climbing trees, and ask yourself what you prefer. It's worth remembering, too, that no one with grown-up children has ever said, 'I wish I'd spent more time watching TV with my kids!'

When is it healthy for children to start watching television?

'My children can start watching one or two specially selected TV programmes a week and using computers when they can read books with enjoyment, hold a conversation, and occupy themselves happily – for example, playing by themselves or with other children', was one parent's answer to this question. Other parents are keen to know what childcare professionals think before making up their minds.

American doctors are now so concerned about the effects of the electronic media that they are laying down guidelines to help parents decide. The American Academy of Pediatrics (AAP) now recommends that children under 2 years old should watch no TV at all, and that older children should have sets removed from their bedrooms so that they can only watch in a social space such as the living room. The AAP further recommends that parents of young children should play with them, rather than expose them to the hazards of TV. Playing, doing puzzles, digging in the dirt – these and similar activities are much healthier for brain development, and for exercising social, emotional, and cognitive skills, say the doctors.

Children's bedrooms should be havens for play, relaxation, reading, and chilling out, without any screens. Parents should also not use TV as an electronic babysitter. As we have already seen, such viewing is bad for children's health, and can stunt their developing brains and bodies. Indeed, the doctors recommend that parents provide a media diary for their children to monitor viewing, and to inform doctors visits.

British paediatricians heartily approved of the AAP advice. Dr Harvey Marcovitch of the Royal College of Paediatrics and Child Health said,

'I couldn't agree more. It is music to my ears … Every instinct within me tells me it is right … small children benefit enormously in interacting with an adult. Almost all programmes are unsuitable for young children, they just can't assimilate what is going on. If you talk with a little child it will reply hesitantly because the formulation of its thoughts is slow. Nearly all cartoons portray a behaviour pattern of hyperactivity, which is something parents worry about in their own children. Each scene switches very, very fast and, although an adult has no trouble in understanding what is going on, there is no way a young child can work out what is happening. It is a kind of infant strobe light.'[1]

The emerging consensus amongst educators, doctors, and child-care professionals in North America is strongly against children using the electronic media at an early age. Thus, for example, the annual *TV-Turnoff Week* during the last week of April is widely supported by the Surgeon General, the American Medical Association, the American Federation of Teachers, the National Association for the Education of Young Children, the National Association of Elementary Schools, the American Psychiatric Association, the Association of Library Service to Children, and the National Parenting Association – to name just a few.

Lieutenant Colonel Dave Grossman is a father who brought his children up TV-free in the early years, and as an expert on the effects of screen violence on behaviour he is keen that his grandchildren benefit too:

'I believe that in an ideal world, children should hold off on watching TV until they can tell the difference between fantasy and reality, and 7 or 8 is about that age. I believe this SO strongly, that I am paying (bribing?) my kids, paying them $1,000 a year toward the grandbaby's college fund, for every year that they promise to raise the grandbabys, TV free, up until they are 7 or 8.'[2]

However, parents are having to go against the grain of modern technological culture when they limit their children's viewing. *The Times* editorial which accompanied the news item about the American Academy of Pediatrics is most revealing. We read that the banning of viewing for under 2's and the removing of sets from bedrooms of older children

' ... represents the gravest challenge to the Western way of life since Coca-Cola tried changing its secret formula ... If television is the soma that keeps everyone happy in La-la land, especially at 6.30 in the morning, it is indeed, for all its faults, a blessing. Toddlers can now press the magic button at 5.45 a.m. and for the rest of the day zap from channel to channel until their lust for life is assuaged.'[3]

At the same time, media companies like Disney are targeting younger and younger children with educational games for babies as young as 9 months of age. Two year olds can learn with Winnie-the-Pooh and 4 year olds get ready for school with Mickey Mouse. Matt Carroll, of UK Disney Interactive, sees no reason why 9-month-old babies should not sit in front of a computer screen for 'short bursts' of interactive play. Carroll himself uses the games as a treat for his 2- and 4-year-old children – so they *must* be all right![4]

In spite of the perception that TV in Britain is not as bad for children as it is in the USA, there are several lone voices in Britain who are taking a strong stand. Dr Sally Ward is the speech therapist who discovered that television is an important factor in delaying children's language development in one in five children. She considers that babies under a year should not watch at all, because they will not learn from it. The background noise from TVs stops them listening and learning as they naturally should, so that by 8 months many babies were not able to recognize common words like 'juice' or 'bricks', and they did not know their own names. Children aged 2–3 should watch no more than an hour a day if at all, because TV prevents them from conversing and taking turns speaking. Children get caught by the colours and flashing lights, can be uninterested in play and toys, with so severe a delay in language development that they 'are likely to be educational failures'. The clear implication is that parents stop using the TV as a babysitter, turn off the set, and speak to and play with their children.[5]

Meanwhile, the British government is very enthusiastic about e-literacy and getting children accustomed to computers in nursery and infants schools before entering primary or grade schools. One example of tiny tots getting an early grounding in IT skills is at Technotots, a nursery in Dundee. Technotots merges the care of pre-school children with learning basic computer skills, e-toys, and special educational software, as well as secure web-cam access for parents. Britain's National Curriculum prescribes a computer in every pre-school and infant classroom.

However, other teachers from some Kindergartens and schools take strong issue with such approaches. Whilst many mainstream teachers keep the electronic media in their place, some schools such as the Rudolf Steiner (Waldorf) schools discourage viewing at home and have no TV or computers in either Kindergartens or in junior-grade classrooms. Teachers try to discuss tactfully with parents of young children how best to make use of the creative education on offer, and parents are thereby informed about the importance of this issue, and are given a clear rationale for limiting their children's access to the electronic media.

The following is a briefing that St Paul's School, Islington, London gives to their parents when their child enters the school:

'Television

TV is embedded in our culture and taken for granted to such a degree that it is often difficult for us to question its value. Similarly, with the increasing prominence of cinema, the personal computer and video games and their adoption into everyday life, rarely is a dissenting voice heard. However it is widely held amongst those involved in Steiner education, as well as by researchers in the USA (see recommended reading), that watching TV and videos and playing computer games is detrimental to the healthy development of the child. Our reasons for this are:

I.   All children have an innate imaginative capacity and their natural state is to be active in this. This is one of the great gifts of childhood and crucial for their healthy journey into adulthood, when children acquire other faculties. As they do so, it is a capacity, which is usually lost or transformed, never to be re-lived in the same way. TV, videos and/or computer games etc. make children unhealthily 'still' and stifle their own imaginations. By presenting the child with 'finished' images, the child is required to do no inner work (or active play) at all and their imagination is 'disabled' whilst watching. Afterwards, this can result in listlessness, lack of initiative and boredom; children may need to be constantly entertained. Alternatively, it may result in children being over-stimulated to such an extent that they can no longer listen properly to real people – they switch on or off as they please. It is felt that this kind of stimulation is in fact deprivation for the child's own abundant creative abilities.

II. Through our education, we encourage children's natural capacity to be highly sensitive to their environment and the people around them. They are, therefore, deeply susceptible to being mesmerised; they cannot filter their absorption of the things they see and hear. We are careful in both the Kindergarten and school to present material in a way appropriate to their age and sensibilities. By contrast, frequently, the quality of children's material on TV, videos and computers is very poor. They force images and noises of all kinds upon the child which are in our view inappropriate – the children may become desensitised as their threshold for violence, noise, aesthetics, moral and social behaviours – you name it – lowers. Young children do not have the discrimination to regulate their own watching. They are not yet able to know what is good for them and what is not, and they depend on the adults around them to decide the boundaries, which will protect them (in all areas of life, not just this one) until they can freely take care of themselves.

III.   Furthermore, the images that flash past on the screen are not connected to real life – they are an artificial representation of life and, as such, abstract. One cannot relate to TV. By contrast, in a Steiner school, the teachers do not use textbooks – they seek to give stories and lesson content from memory so that the communication exchange is real and alive. Children live vividly in the present and to be healthy they need to feel deeply connected to the world around them. They do not have the intellectual sophistication to cope healthily with this abstract phenomenon. TV et al. literally undo the work we do at our school.

We would ideally like all TVs to be gathering dust under a cloth in the cupboard or to be thrown away completely. However, recognising that this is unlikely we request that children attending St Paul's do not watch TV from Sunday to Thursday. They should definitely not watch TV in the mornings before coming to school.

If your child is used to a heavy diet of television watching, don't despair! It may be easier than it sounds to change your family routine. Many of us have discovered that one-time TV addicts have found a wealth of positive things to do in the creative and supportive atmosphere of a Steiner school community.'

Whilst the St Paul's School teachers are very clear about why they are inviting parents to limit their child's viewing at home, they are also concerned to be open and give information so parents can make up their own minds. School administrator Jane Gerhard says that, 'Basically we talk about it seriously at the open parents evenings that parents have to attend before their child is admitted and address it again at interview. There is also an article about the electronic media in the parents' handbook' (see above).

Jane continues:

'We have found by putting our foot down we have caused parents to lie to us, and to tell their children not to talk about what they have seen. This is not a productive relationship. Also what do we intend to do about it … expel the child? Haul the parents over the coals and act like moral policemen?

I have just recently had the experience of a young mum – a trainee social worker when interviewed, and now qualified.

"You know Janet, when you told me about TV at the interview 3 years ago I decided I would have to prove it for myself. Well I want you to know that you were right. Last night before Cameron fell asleep he was singing all the French and German songs that he has been learning in Class One. It was then that I realized that he would not have done that had he watched TV beforehand. Thanks so much."'

Conclusion: The Older that Children Use the Electronic Media, the Better!

Dorothy Cohen, a respected American educator, was an early advocate of restricting TV-viewing:

'The impact of television on so-called disadvantaged children has been minimal in terms of goals such as learning to read – but its impact on their development has been great. It has robbed them of their normal opportunities to talk, to play, to *do*. It has interfered with their normal opportunities to grow. The big thing for me is the protection of children during the period of vulnerability in their lives. I think children under five should not watch television at all.'[6]

Joan Almon, US co-ordinator of the Alliance for Childhood, tells the story of two girls who were comparing their respective dolls. One girl's doll was electronically enhanced, and she boasted, 'My doll can say 500 words!' The other girl had a well-worn cloth doll and retorted, 'My doll can say anything I want her to say!'

In the course of comprehensively reviewing the effects of the electronic media on young children, it becomes clear that those who are pushing the interests of the electronic media have forgotten – or are ignoring – the basic development needs of children. Parenting becomes product development, and children are the products. One such 'child product' is 6-year-old Lily, who precociously observes that:

> 'Britney's a role model. She's fashionable, and she has movements that I like. My mom won't let me wear what I want, because she's bossy. I really like belly shirts. It's an ordinary T-shirt, but it shows your belly. I really want to be a teenager. Now. Teenagers dress up cool, so boys like them. I saw it in a movie. They get dressed so fashionable, like a doll and stuff. I want to be on television, so everyone can see my pretty face and my whole body. I love girls. They rock. And they rule. And boys drool.'[7]

Dr Jane Healy is an educational psychologist, with over 30 years' experience as an educator, researcher, and mother. Her two groundbreaking books *Endangered Minds* (1990) and *Failure to Connect* (1998) offer a very thoroughly researched analysis of the effects on children under bombardment from a fast-paced media culture. On the basis of her research she recommends, in a nutshell, that *children under 7 years of age should not use TV or computers.* After that, the electronic media should be sensitively integrated with the curriculum, ensuring good planning and that the reasons for use are intellectually valid. She recommends not spending money on computers until other educational essentials have been met, such as the arts, reading and maths specialists, physical space, a library, small classes, and well-trained teachers. If computers are used, teachers can be trained in their use as part of the curriculum, but no 'educational software' or games should be used.[8]

Thomas Poplawski summarizes the view of many Steiner (Waldorf) school teachers on when to start watching and using computers:

'Parents may succeed in protecting a child from the media. There is then the question as to how long this should continue. Among Waldorf teachers, responses to this question reflect a continuum from a purist position – that to some is impractical and unenforceable – through levels of compromise in bowing to what is felt to be an unstoppable force of popular culture. Almost all teachers feel there should be no media at all before age seven. Some put this at age nine. Many then are willing to countenance judicious use of television between ages nine and twelve, with parents ideally watching along with their children. Many teachers feel that after the onset of adolescence the young person should have freedom in this area but also the benefit of parental guidance.

Still, something quite subtle may be compromised in the development of the child. Roberto Trostli is a Waldorf teacher who has taken several classes through the upper elementary grades. He comments that among graduating eighth graders, he can tell which ones still have little or no exposure to media. They are the self-starters and the children in the class with the most initiative. Such an observation may be the most compelling reason for parents to take a hard look at the media question.'[9]

The best way to combat the hazards of the electronic media is to exclude screen culture from children's lives as much as possible for *at least* the first seven years. The electronic media are powerful drugs, like alcohol or tobacco, so children need protection from them until they can decide for themselves without getting hooked. And until then, children need all their energy to learn to walk, speak and think, to move, play games, enjoy nature, to exercise the imagination, to mess around, to be bored, and to engage in spontaneous, creative play. The compelling maxim emerging from this discussion could go something like this: 'No more remote-controlled, overscheduled childhood, and no more bedroom screen culture – but rather, let us champion the reclaiming of a childhood that is rapidly being lost to technological culture.'

But what are the practical means by which we can cope with the electronic media, such that families can control rather than be taken over by them? This is the topic of the next chapter.

In a Nutshell ...

1. The electronic media make good servants, but bad masters. So when is it OK for children to start watching and using the electronic media?
2. Researchers offer varying advice: Dr Sally Ward recommends not before at least one year old, and then carefully used. The American Association of Pediatrics recommends no media use before the age of 2. Researcher Jane Healy says preferably not before age 7.
3. Schools and Kindergartens with cautious electronic media policies, such as Steiner (Waldorf) schools, mostly recommend no electronic media use at home or at school before the age of 7, and then very limited amounts until 9–12 years. Steiner schools are unusual in that teachers are alert to the issues, though they are conscious of going against the grain of a popular cultural trend in suggesting limits to electronic media use.

4. Every family has the choice of making up its own mind – every child and situation is unique, and there are no easy solutions.

5. It takes will and persistence to protect today's children from the powerful commercial conditioning delivered via the electronic media, as in the example of Lily, the 'fast-forwarded' child media 'product'.

9. Limiting Exposure to the Electronic Media

The most important thing we've learned,
So far as children are concerned,
Is never, NEVER, *NEVER,* let
Them near your television set -
Or better still, just don't install
The idiotic thing at all.

From 'Advice on Television' by Roald Dahl,
from *Charlie and the Chocolate Factory*

The aim of this chapter is to offer practical coping strategies so that you will be able to choose what is right for you and your children. This will result in your taking control of the electronic media within your family environment. The focus will be on the first seven years, as these are the most important for child development. As the Jesuits used to say, if you educate children for the first seven years, then you have laid the foundations for their whole lives. 'All I ever learned was in the Kindergarten!' Some strategies and tips will be offered for older families, as well as to those wishing to cut down on electronic media use.

Preventing Electronic Addiction in the Early Years

A sound basis for success in coping with the electronic media will be laid if you and your partner can discuss and regularly review the situation at home, both before you have children and whilst they are growing up. It is much easier to *prevent* electronic addiction in the early years than to tackle it later!

A first step is to discuss with your partner what you see as the effects of the media on children, and your children's needs. Then, if you are both agreed that you will not expose your baby or young children to TV, computers, and video games until an agreed age, such as 7, then you will have laid the solid foundation for a shared approach and strategy.

Making the choice to delay your children's exposure to the electronic media until an appropriate age, to know when to turn off the set, and to use the internet only for specifically circumscribed purposes, are all very important. It will mean that you have chosen a more active family life – where you like to play with your children, tell them stories, make things, enjoy nature, draw, and do household tasks together. Whilst your children will be much more likely to occupy themselves constructively, there may well still be times, such as at 'rush hour' in the late afternoon, when you are cooking, with your children perhaps tired and argumentative, when you wished you did have the equivalent of an electronic babysitter!

However, when the thought of '*video or TV as electronic babysitter*' does cross your mind, you can remind yourself of the 'vicious viewing cycle' – i.e. that the more children watch, the more they become tele-addicts and the less able they are to play by themselves. Children are by nature active, curious, inventive, and playful; so when you provide a dressing-up clothes box, a playhouse, a nature table, an art corner, and games and simple toys, they will soon find something to do. Making conscious, clear choices about media use works; it is the first step to getting a more creative family life. Helen tells the story of how she decided to have a TV-free home:

'Ruth is 11 now and had the first six years of her life without a TV. It all started while I was reading *Who's Bringing Them Up?* by Martin Large. I read the story of the little girl who was watching a woman cooking on television. The girl tried to get into the screen to take part in the activity. She then went out into the kitchen where her mother was cooking, only to be told to go back and watch television. I didn't want that to happen to Ruth. I was deeply impressed by the description of how we go into sleep mode when we watch the screen. I wanted a child who would be alert, creative, and interested.

About half way through the book I sold our TV. It was re-introduced into our house when my brother came to live with us. We now have the option of joining him on the top floor to watch a film or programme. Ruth can now plan and cook a three-course meal, making up some of the recipes, and has grown up to be independent, interesting, and alert. She is easily frightened as she has a vivid imagination, and images on the screen are often too much for her. On the other hand, she is a wonderful story-teller. Her attention span is excellent and she rarely says, "I'm bored". If she does, I suggest she goes and makes something. Her favourite activity used to be "making". Her favourite activity now is playing with her friends.

Our lifestyle may be unusual, but I think the biggest influence on Ruth and I, apart from home education, has been her early years without the influence and incredible time-taking of television.

The biggest thing I notice about my home without a TV is the calm atmosphere. People often comment on what a sanctuary it may seem to be and how peaceful they feel when they come there.'

Helen's story is one of many, as increasing numbers of families are deciding to limit the exposure of their children to the electronic media. Even media celebrities such as Madonna, Tom Cruise, and Steven Spielberg are keen to set limits. Madonna wants 'minimal TV' for her children. Tom Cruise, with two school-age children says, 'I don't really like my kids watching that much television. They are allowed about three and a half hours a week, but only if they are doing well in school. We're focused on reading, a lot of reading.' He continues, ' I don't really like to leave them alone on computers – I am not convinced it is healthy for them.'

Steven Spielberg and Kate Capshaw have five children. He says that one hour of viewing is enough, but only if the conditions have been met, such as homework, and finishing dinner and household chores. And given the terrifying TV news images of the 9/11 World Trade Centre collapse, Spielberg doesn't let his children watch the news: 'I do not let them watch the news because it is much more uncensored than it was when I was growing up, and things are so frightening right now that I like the news to come from me. That way I can reassure them that they are safe.'[1]

The small but significant trend amongst parents to cut down on viewing, with 'no-TV days', or no TV at all in their children's early years, is resulting in fitter children, better schoolwork, and improved general well-being. A Kaiser Family Foundation report found that when children cut down their viewing, they were happier, and showed gains both at school and in relationships – 'The best recipe for happiness we have seen without medication for years'.[2]

Far from the limiting of children's use of the electronic media being weird or unusual, then, it is something which increasing numbers of parents are struggling with – and successfully. The easiest way to set limits, though, is certainly to keep the electronic media out of your children's way for the first seven years.

Where to Keep Your TV and Computers

It's a good idea for you and your partner to consider where to keep your electronic media hardware before your first child is even born. Computers and television are helpful servants, but bad masters. Right from the start, you can keep your computer in your bedroom, office, garden shed, or work room – well away from where your child is likely to be. One place for the television is in your bedroom so you can choose to watch it away from the children; or it can be housed in the living-room under a cloth or in a cabinet with the video, where it can be kept out of sight when not in use. A television set in the kitchen is an invitation to watch during meal-times! Out of sight, out of mind …

This will then commonly lead into a discussion of how to handle noise levels in the house, bearing in mind Sally Ward's research (referred to earlier) on the effects in the child's early years of background noise from radios and CD players as well as from TVs. The aim is to create a relaxing, peaceful environment at home. Young children's sleep problems will often disappear when there is no constant background noise.

It is tempting to introduce lullaby cassettes or CDs with nursery rhymes, or even to use a favourite video before bed when your child gets older. However, singing your baby to sleep yourself, singing nursery rhymes together, or telling stories before sleep is both more fun and a much better way of calming your child so they can sleep – not to mention the other manifold benefits that such real human relating will furnish.

It is important to be aware of your friends' and relatives' well-intentioned inclination to shower your young family with inappropriate computer games, videos, TV-related toys, or even the occasional TV or PC for your child! For some reason, as soon as people know that you make only a cautious use of TV in the family, they tend to think that you are depriving the children. However, if people do feel generous, then books, age-related games, and simple toys such as bricks, balls, or cloth dolls are much more appropriate than expensive, highly sophisticated toys that leave nothing to the imagination. Tact and sensitivity are obviously sometimes needed to explain your approach to toys and play. I usually suggested that we were a bit old-fashioned! In our family, inappropriate toys were quietly weeded out, and then forgotten on top shelves until they ended up in a jumble sale.

As your baby gets older, you have the chance to redesign areas of your home for their activities. It's important to be prepared for a 'creative mess' – the price of active children can be an untidy house, even though you can clear it up together as a game before tea-time! What follows are suggestions about the basics for encouraging your child to have a healthy, natural childhood.

A play space – a play area with dressing-up clothes, a basket of dolls, puppets, dolls house, or a barn and a Wendy house. A special place where children can play, sometimes out of your sight, such as a play-corner, a space under the stairs – a space that is theirs. Don't forget as a parent, the joys of 'floor-time', when you get down on the floor with your child and play imaginatively. These include rough-and-tumble games – rolling around and having a good laugh – whilst making sure your child also feels safe and respects vulnerabilities. Sally Jenkinson, in her well-observed book *The Genius of Play*, writes of how children need a parent's 'licence' or permission to play. She describes the many ways in which children play, and how they can enjoy free unstructured creative play for long periods.[3]

Toys – Children are very happy playing with simple toys, such as a piece of knotted cloth for a doll, and a rough face drawn on the knot representing the head. You can take a great deal of care in choosing toys – simple toys that invite imagination are more fun than expensive licensed toys that are so 'perfect' that play is difficult. Licensed toys are linked with TV shows and films books, and usually have just a single purpose. Open-ended toys like blocks, play dough, and clay, on the other hand, are much more fun. A child can be just as happy kicking a squashed can with a friend as an expensive ball, or playing with a cardboard box, rather than the expensive toy.

A nature table – for young children to re-create the season, with flowers, fruits, fossils, crystals, moss, a bird's nest, plants, and candles. The nature table can become the focus for celebrating seasonal festivals, for bringing back nature's treasures from walks, and for pictures of seasonal happenings. It is a way of connecting with nature, important in both urban and rural areas. The book *The Children's Year* gives helpful instructions about how to make nature tables.[4]

A sports area – a box or a cupboard, with balls, bats, ropes, skipping-ropes, skates, rackets – for ball games, hopscotch, etc. See Kim Payne's *Games Children Play*[5] for ideas for games with children appropriate to their age. There are co-operative games, and also games for parties.

An art and craft table – a table or area where children can paint, draw, make things, use play-dough, sew, knit, make models. There are crayons, paper, card, aprons, wool, glue, cloths, rags, scissors, pencils, and brushes, which are all sorted into boxes, jars, and baskets of assorted sizes. Try making presents for birthdays and festivals. It is remarkable to see how often children gravitate to a craft table – and once you have shown how to get started, the children will really want to continue!

Celebrate festivals with your children, starting with special days such as birthdays. Observing the seasonal round of festivals is an enjoyable way of marking the year, and children soon start looking forward to the next festival with eager anticipation. Each festival involves making things, creating nature tables, telling stories, making food, singing songs, and playing games. At Christmas, resource books like *Festivals, Family,* and *Food*[6] offer a rich range of festive ideas that children love and look forward to.

A music area – this may be a piano, or a corner in the living-room where there are instruments such as drums, tambourines, recorders, a simple lyre, and music, and where one can play music by oneself or with others. Having instruments like recorders and guitars around encourages children to become interested in playing. Regular singing at bedtimes, meal-times with graces, at festivals, or at story-time during the day gets you into the habit of singing through the day and through the year.

Garden play space – You can make sure that there's a good sandpit, swing, climbing frame, playhouse, and a play area if you have a garden or can share garden space with your neighbour. Gardening with young children is important – for example, if they each have a small garden they can plant bulbs and seeds in it, and tend them with you throughout the year, so that your children get their hands dirty! Otherwise, tending window boxes and plant pots is an alternative, as well as sprouting seeds and plant pots with bulbs on the nature table.

Stories and books – Create a children's book corner, with shelves, reading space, a warm carpet, rug, and pillows, to curl up with an age-appropriate book, starting with big picture books with little or no print in them. Reading books can be a delight, but you yourself telling stories is what your children will really love. You are the best story-teller in the world to them – whether it's nursery rhymes, singing songs, telling them the story of their day, repetitive stories like Goldilocks, or fairy stories and picture story books. If you don't feel that confident as a singer, try joining a local community choir, or take a story-telling course! Remember what Albert Einstein said about story-telling, 'If you want your children to be clever, tell them stories. If you want them to be wise, tell them even more stories!'

Meal-times – Make sure you share meals together, with the TV and radio off, so you can talk about the day ahead if it's breakfast, or what's happened that day if it's supper. Conversation around the table is the heart of family life, where children learn how to take turns at speaking, where stories are told, and you just enjoy being together.

Bedtimes – Bedtimes are special for both parents and children. This is a time for tidying up your child's bedroom with them, making sure their clothes are ready for the next day, sharing the story of the day, talking though anything bothering your child, looking forward to the next day, telling a story, and singing a lullaby while giving a back rub, ending with a good-night verse or prayer. Such bedtime rituals are very calming for children, so they look forward to going to bed and are ready for sleep. If you are a busy parent, it may be the one time in the day when *you* can relax, let go, and just *be* with your child – though it's easy for you to go to sleep as well!

Games evening – Set aside one evening a week for indoor games and develop a family games repertoire.

Cooking and other activities – Try cooking simple meals with your children so that when they are old enough they can cook meals for you all once a week, go out to play sports regularly such as learning to swim, go for walks, take up a hobby, have another family over, take the children to the library or on other educational or fun visits. The problem is how to find a balance in all this, and to find a rhythm that works for you and your family, without falling into the trap of over-scheduling. Your job is not to entertain your children, but to provide a nurturing home where your children can find their own rhythm – suffering from neither over-stimulation nor neglect.

Boredom – Modern life is so pressurized, there is little time to stand and stare. So when our children say they are bored, give them time for day-dreaming and boredom. Hold back on too much structure! When there is nothing scheduled to do, children will usually find ways of occupying themselves. This often leads to the creative, unstructured play that is essential for and nourishes children's growth. If the materials and play-space are at hand, children will soon start making something, or begin to initiate their own play.

These young family activities are just the beginning. There are many helpful resource books to consult when you have questions. You can share ideas and activities with your friends who have their own young children, and your child's nursery, playgroup, or Kindergarten may have parent craft classes. Having a young family will keep parents very busy, but at the same time it is very rewarding and satisfying.

Visits to Friends' Homes

Whilst you can keep your own children 'screen-free', what happens when they play at friends' houses? If you are clear about why you have chosen to limit your child's electronic media exposure, then when asked by other parents you can tell them. It is becoming much more accepted now for parents to agree ground rules for visits. One father suggests to the host parent, 'Please do send our children home if your child starts watching TV or playing computer games; I'd prefer it if they just played!' This kind of strategy usually works well. Sometimes, even if the other family knows you'd prefer no TV for your child, it does sometimes happen. Although it's not the end of the world, you can try saying that whilst you appreciate the invitation to play, because TV can have negative effects you would prefer your child definitely not to watch next time they go to play. Then you can also agree ground rules with your child, like suggesting alternatives to viewing such as going outside to play, or making something together.

After a while, you will tend to build up a circle of families with a similar approach to play – where you know your children can go to visit without the intrusion of the electronic media. In my own family we found that many visiting children, who had a high diet of TV and computer games, really preferred just playing.

What Happens when You Limit the Electronic Media?

There will be far more creative activity in your home when you limit the electronic media. It certainly tends to be noisier with more active play – whether it's bricks falling down, water play inside or outside, or music practice. The house will be messier, with play things all over the family room, mud tracked in, or children wanting to play near you. There will be far more activity – games, cooking, making playhouses, playing hide and seek. You will be more occupied with children's interests such as going to the library, the local park, a nature reserve, cycling to friends – but they will get healthily tired. At the same time as you *save* money on expensive computer games, it's worth remembering that trips, outings, and sports activities can also sometimes be expensive.

Children will talk more, play for longer, be less demanding for junk foods, know how to occupy themselves, do their household chores, sleep better, and be more geared up to learning skills such as playing an instrument or learning a sport – and they will be more relaxed. I remember some old neighbours telling me that our children 'played just like old-fashioned children – for a long time, totally absorbed, and it looked so interesting, what they were doing!'.

Almost the final word in this chapter can be left with Roald Dahl:

'Advice on Television' by Roald Dahl

> The most important thing we've learned,
> So far as children are concerned,
> Is never, NEVER, *NEVER,* let
> Them near your television set -
> Or better still, just don't install
> The idiotic thing at all. In almost every house we've been,
> We've watched them gaping at the screen.
> They loll and slop and lounge about,
> And stare until their eyes pop out.
> (Last week in someone's place we saw
> A dozen eyeballs on the floor.)

They sit and stare and stare and sit
Until they're hypnotized by it,
Until they're absolutely drunk
With all that shocking ghastly junk.
Oh yes, we know it keeps them still,
They don't climb out the window sill,
They never fight or kick or punch,
They leave you free to cook the lunch
And wash the dishes in the sink -
But did you ever stop to think,
To wonder just exactly what
This does to your beloved tot?
IT ROTS THE SENSES IN THE HEAD!
IT KILLS IMAGINATION DEAD!
IT CLOGS AND CLUTTERS UP THE MIND!
IT MAKES A CHILD SO DULL AND BLIND.
HE CAN NO LONGER UNDERSTAND
A FANTASY, A FAIRYLAND!
HIS BRAIN BECOMES AS SOFT AS CHEESE!
HIS POWERS OF THINKING RUST AND FREEZE!
HE CANNOT THINK – HE ONLY SEES!

But what about the next step, when children reach 7 and enter Year, Class or Grade 1? How can families with older children cope with the electronic media? When can children actually start using TV and computers with comparative safety?

In a Nutshell …

1. The easiest time to limit exposure is when your children are young – in the first seven years.

2. You can re-arrange where you put the TV and PC in your home, so as to keep the TV and PC out of the way of your children.
3. Toddlers and young children are active, curious, and enjoy playing – so if you provide a nurturing space for play, exercise, and activities, they will learn how to occupy themselves well.
4. Be prepared to be active yourself – it's tempting to use TV as an electronic babysitter, but it only undermines children's ability to occupy themselves.
5. You are not your child's entertainment manager! If they are bored, then there is enough around for them to decide what to do next.
6. Simple, open toys like a dressing-up box or bricks engage children most. One experiment showed that when all their toys were taken away from a group of Kindergarten-age children, they soon invented replacements from very basic everyday objects.
7. A rhythm to the day – e.g. of getting up, meal-times, walks/ outdoor activities, story-times – really helps to provide safety and structure, so that, for example, your children look forward to bedtime as a special time.
8. Visiting and playing at other homes needs tact and assertiveness in agreeing ground rules about not watching or not using computer games. More and more people understand and respect the families who place clear limits on media exposure.
9. Your children will benefit from being more secure, happy, and creative than many toddlers and preschoolers exposed to a high electronic media diet. They will have a childhood. In spite of the challenges of being a more active parent, you will treasure your young family years. You will never say, 'I wish I'd played more computer games and watched more TV when my children were young!'

10. Coping Strategies for Families with Older Children (7 and over)

'All right!' you'll cry. 'All right!' you'll say,
'But if we take the set away,
What shall we do to entertain?
Our darling children! Please explain!'
We'll answer this by asking you,
'What used the darling ones to do?
How used they keep themselves contented
Before this monster was invented?'
Have you forgotten? Don't you know?
We'll say it very loud and slow:
THEY ...USED ...TO ...READ! They'd READ and READ,
AND READ and READ, AND THEN PROCEED
To READ, some more. Great Scott! Gadzooks!
One half their lives was reading books!

'Advice on Television' by Roald Dahl

Constructive Coping for Families with Older Children

Given the pressures of modern life, and also the undoubted benefits that can accrue from the electronic media when sensibly used, it is important to consider when it is appropriate for children over 7 years old to start using TVs and computers in the home. Many mainstream schools make regular use of the electronic media, so unless there is the choice of an appropriate screen-free grade or junior school, parents need to consider how best to cope in the family.

Each family will make its own choice about how to tackle this challenging question. If you have developed a creative, active family life in the first seven years, then you can at least try introducing TV or computers when it feels appropriate. Apart from an initial novelty effect, you may find that your children are so engaged with normal family activities, friends, and play that they're not that interested.

For some parents, values are important in guiding for this decision. Thus, for example, some religious groups such as the Quakers, or people who don't like the levels of violence on TV and computer games, will exercise strong control over programme content. Parents worried about the overwhelming effects of commercialization will limit exposure until their children are critically aware and can choose to turn off. Others will be much more concerned about child health and well-being. Some parents, having read the arguments of the psychologists Fred and Merrelyn Emery, or of Jane Healy (all discussed earlier), consider that the human brain is fundamentally maladapted to the CRT/VDT medium. They will therefore be very reluctant to have *their* children exposed to the electronic media before they are teenagers. This is generally the considered view of many Waldorf (Rudolf Steiner) School teachers. They also emphasize how the CRT blunts the senses, the imagination, and the capacity for independent thinking, and that limiting media exposure is important for healthy child development.

Other parents decide that certain conditions must be met before allowing their child to use a PC or watch TV. Such conditions include the ability to read books with enjoyment, to write, to concentrate, to carry our regular household chores, to have a hobby or regular sport, to play, or the capacity to occupy themselves for a reasonable time.

Reading is important because it is the first and foremost children's activity that gets displaced by the electronic media. It is also the key to educational success for children, according to recent research. *Reading for Change* found that the enthusiasm of children for reading frequently in the home had a much bigger effect on their educational success than their families' wealth or social class.[1] However, if you answer 'yes' to a number of the following questions, then allowing your child to use the electronic media may well lead to a deterioration of their behaviour in a whole range of ways:

- How much does your child require instant gratification? Is there a low tolerance of frustration?
- Is your child hyperactive, lacking in self-control, overactive with behaviour problems, aggressive? Can he or she sit still for a story or a game?
- Does your child get on with other children?
- Does s/he carry out regular household tasks?
- Are there nightmares, anxieties, and fears that make sleep difficult?
- How well does your child express herself?
- Is your child bored a lot, finding it hard to amuse himself or to play?
- Is paying attention and the ability to concentrate difficult?

If you are concerned about your child's behaviour and learning difficulties after considering the above check-list, it could be useful to have a discussion with your child's teacher, a special learning needs advisor, or an educational psychologist. Whilst TV and computer games will occupy your child, overall they may make your child's behaviour worse if the root causes are not resolved.

Different approaches to coping with the electronic media

Clear limits to media use, with agreed ground rules

Many parents, like Tom Cruise, offer their school-age child the choice of one or two specially selected programmes each week. They disagree with limiting viewing to one or two hours every day, as this is habit forming, so the making of conscious, positive choices is encouraged. One family with three boys chooses to watch 'Ready, Steady, Cook' together. As a result their two older boys aged 9 and 7 are keen to cook at dinner parties. The programme inspired them to cook – which certainly pleased their parents! The other programme they chose was 'Scrapheap Challenge', which was so good for technical knowledge that one child could explain just how a clockwork car worked.

This family keeps a 14-inch TV set and video recorder under a cloth in their living room, with the father occasionally using a laptop at home for work. The rules for the older boys are a maximum of two hours viewing a week (never on school days), and occasionally a video treat – such as old-fashioned videos at their Gran's. When these children play at neighbours' houses and the parents say 'Our kids don't watch TV', the neighbours say, 'Oh yes, we understand – this is a Steiner-Waldorf thing!' But families with children in mainstream schools, and home educators, may need to have an online PC with a printer at home, for example for accessing information on the web for homework. The common solution seems to be to have the PC in the hall-way, living-room, or social space – so all family members can use it, and so that parents can also supervise computer use.

The danger is that when children have computers in their bedrooms, they can easily use them unsupervised for long periods of time. It can suit working parents to have their children away from the living area, because it is less disruptive if you have teen-agers. An extreme example of this behaviour is the Japanese teenage boys who retreat to their screen-stuffed bedrooms for years, only to emerge at night for food! One education tutor who visits students at home tells parents that they are wasting their time and money by letting their teenager bury themselves in their bedroom with their PC. He commonly observes immediate educational gains when the PC comes down from the bedroom into the living-room or into the hall-way.

Other families allow TV or computer games during the week on school days, but never just after coming home from school and not until chores and homework have been done. Active families also tend to find that electronic media use declines sharply as spring and summer arrive.

Many families decide on some ground rules for guiding media use.

A sample framework of ground rules for electronic media use

There is much common ground about using the electronic media, although every family needs to agree its own rules and review them from time to time. Families can try discussing and deciding which ones are useful for their particular situation:

1. The electronic media are normally off limits for all children of 7 years and under, or whenever you choose to set the age limit.

For school age children:

2. No electronic media use on school days – but if you do agree on watching a specially selected programme, not before homework or chores have been done. And certainly no breakfast TV on school days!
3. No TVs or PCs in bedrooms. Limit your family to one TV/video set in the living-room, in a cabinet or under a cloth. Keep the PC in the hall-way or a room where all the family have access to it.

4. If you allow, say, an hour a day of viewing or computer games, then this may become a habit; so invite your children to choose specific programmes or games, and set a time limit. Viewing limited to children's or special-interest programmes only. Viewing by young children only when adults are present – and the news will need monitoring. Programmes must be switched off promptly at the end.

5. Discuss how you can best use the PC for information, games, e-mail, and chat rooms when your children are ready – and learn how to use them together.

6. Balance PC and TV use with physical exercise – so for every hour of viewing, consider having *two* hours of physical exercise, so as to avoid becoming a couch potato or vid-kid. (One father only let his children watch if they rode an exercise bike which generated enough electricity to run the TV set!)

7. Avoid buying TV-related magazines, toys, products, and newspapers.

8. Make viewing or PC use a conscious choice – so don't switch on and channel surf, hoping for something interesting, but choose in advance. Similarly with web surfing.

9. Make sure you take health precautions with the seating arrangements for PCs: check the ergonomics, use eye tests, check for back pains and musculo-skeletal problems – if in doubt, ask the advice of an optometrist, a doctor, etc.; also, take safety precautions about potential abuses of the Internet – for example, screening out violent, pornographic, or intrusive content (see Appendix 1). There are many software filters available for this purpose.[2]

Jim Trelease, in *The Read Aloud Handbook*, tells the story of how his family developed their own rules for viewing. When the Treleases first announced to their two children that viewing was to be restricted, they started to cry – and continued to be upset on and off for four months. The reason for limited viewing was that their 9-year-old daughter and 5-year-old son were showing signs of TV addiction. Each night's customary 'read aloud' time was deteriorating because the children said, 'It took too much time away from the TV'. Another factor was seeing how some friends had no TV on weekdays for their four children – and the manifold advantages that accrued as a result. The Treleases had to withstand peer-group pressure from their children's friends, and from other parents. 'And what about the National Geographic Specials?', they would say.

After three months of the new TV regime, there was enough time for reading aloud, for books, for unhurried homework, for games, for cooking, for model making, letter writing, sports, painting, drawing, household jobs – and, 'best of all, to talk with each other, ask questions, and answer questions … Our children's imaginations were coming back to life again'. Their TV plan was as follows:

- The television is turned off at supper-time and not turned on again, Monday to Thursday.
- Each child is allowed to watch one school-night show a week (subject to parents' approval). Homework, chores, etc. must be completed beforehand.
- Weekend television is limited to any two of the three nights. The remaining night is reserved for homework and other activities. The children make their selections separately.

The selection encouraged discriminating viewing and their children became very choosy. They either forgot the option of a special programme during the week, or chose not to watch. However, Trelease observed that: 'If you are going to require children to curtail their TV viewing, if you are going to create a three-hour void in their daily lives, then you must make a commitment to fill that void.'[3]

So it is important to review your family media use regularly with your partner and children – to keep up with changing needs, to discuss the reasons for choices, and to develop critical media literacy so your children develop the ability to make their own choices. We used to have a family gathering with our four children on Sunday evenings, for reading a story, and then looking ahead at the week. This was a good time to decide what we wanted to do.

There are many advantages to be gained with rationing access to the electronic media for children aged 7–12 years of age. They will learn how to use the media responsibly, when you and they feel they are ready. There will be no 'forbidden fruit', leading to subsequent overuse to compensate. Normal family activities, such as the encouragement of reading, will usually crowd out the electronic media. You will be able to censor and restrict the computer games that are clearly designed to hook children, and choose more suitable ones if appropriate. Your children will be able to switch off. They will be able to share a little of the special programmes they watch with friends at school so they do not feel so unusual. And, depending on the individual child, like Roald Dahl, they may come to 'love you for what you did'.

In a Nutshell ...

1. The choice about when to introduce TV and computers into family life for the over 7s depends on your values about programme content, your views on the effects of the CRT/VDT medium on child growth and the brain, and the needs of individual children.
2. If you are concerned about your child's behaviour and learning difficulties, TV and/or computers may well be a factor, so consult with the relevant educators or health professionals.
3. Schools may require children to use computers and the Internet, and some will argue that the interactive nature of computer games is educational – for example, simulations, puzzles, role plays ... Again, it's a decision about what is appropriate in a given situation.

4. Families have different strategies for keeping the media in their useful place – e.g. clear limits to media use, with ground rules. It's useful to develop your own rules – there is no best way.

5. You are not alone: most parents are concerned about cutting down the time their children spend on screen, and many families find that life is so full anyway that they choose carefully what they want from the media. Neil Postman calls this the 'monastery effect', practised by the parents who control the media's access to their children, and create a lively family culture which is both unique and substantially different from the fast-paced media-dominated world.

6. Postman advocates the limiting of media exposure, and he also suggests that we monitor carefully – by watching, using programmes, playing computer games, surfing together – providing a continuously running critique of the values and content. Such attempts at media literacy help educate children to discriminate, so that they can be more able to make their own responsible choices.[4]

'Advice on television' by Roald Dahl

'All right!' you'll cry. 'All right!' you'll say,
'But if we take the set away,
What shall we do to entertain?
Our darling children! Please explain!'
We'll answer this by asking you,
'What used the darling ones to do?
How used they keep themselves contented
Before this monster was invented?'
Have you forgotten? Don't you know?
We'll say it very loud and slow:

THEY...USED ...TO ...READ! They'd READ and READ,
AND READ and READ, AND THEN PROCEED
To READ, some more. Great Scott! Gadzooks!
One half their lives was reading books!
The nursery shelves held books galore!
Books cluttered up the nursery floor!
And in the bedroom, by the bed,
More books were waiting to be read!
Such wondrous, fine fantastic tales
Of dragons, gypsies, queens, and whales
And treasure isles, and distant shores
Where smugglers rowed with muffled oars,
And pirates wearing purple pants,
And sailing ships and elephants,
And cannibals crouching round the pot,
Stirring away at something hot.
Oh, books, what books they used to know,
Those children living long ago!
So please, oh please, we beg, we pray,
Go throw your TV set away,
And in its place you can install
A lovely bookshelf on the wall.
Then fill the shelves with lots of books,
Ignoring all the dirty looks,
The screams and yells, the bites and kicks,
And children hitting you with sticks –
Fear not, because we promise you
That, in about a week or two
Of having nothing else to do,
They'll now begin to feel the need
Of having something good to read.
And once they start – oh boy, oh boy!
You watch the slowly growing joy

That fills their hearts.
They'll grow so keen
They'll wonder what they'd ever seen
In that ridiculous machine,
That nauseating, foul, unclean,
Repulsive television screen!
And later, each and every kid
Will love you more for what you did.

Copyright © Roald Dahl 1964
Reprinted with the author's kind permission.[5]

11. Reclaiming Childhood for Children

A growing number of parents and educators are advocating that childhood be reclaimed from aggressive commercialization, from doing too much too soon at school, from the over-stimulation of the electronic media and from social isolation in the home in multimedia dominated bedrooms. In Britain, rising numbers of children are afraid to play outdoors, as the once secure social spaces of their neighbourhoods are perceived to be dangerous. In 1971, eight out of ten 8 year olds walked to school, but by 1997 it was just one in ten. Media panics about stranger-danger or paedophiles only compound these anxieties, as did the repeat showings of the 9/11 attacks on the World Trade Centre – which Steve Evans of the BBC graphically termed 'pornographic' as some image sequences were shown repeatedly with music, and as an unnecessary backdrop to talking heads.[1]

In a recent study, child mental health researchers discovered that one in five children were suffering from anxiety and depression; 12 per cent had anxiety disorders, 10 per cent disruptive disorders, 5 per cent attention deficit disorders, and 6 per cent developmental disorders. The recent Mental Health Foundation Report, *Bright Futures*, likened childhood to a war zone of family breakdowns, rising school demands, fear about outdoor play, fractured neighbourhoods, and loss of hope in the future.

Peter Wilson of Young Minds, a children's mental health organization, reflected on the loss of childhood:

'Technology – TV, film, computers – has blasted all of that away. It has dissolved the differences. Whereas children used to have to qualify to become adults, by learning how to read, for example, anyone can consume TV … It's not so much the diminishing of childhood innocence, but the fading of childhood as gradual development, gradual discovery … Childhood is rushed now, chivvied up beyond the proper pace … Children are not as resilient as we think.'[2]

Yet we also live at a very creative time, when families, schools, and communities can join together in protecting and reclaiming childhood. To give just one example, whilst writing this book I was visiting the seaside town of St Ives in the far south-west of England. Weather permitting, children and teenagers came out in numbers after school, with skate-boarders excelling at incredible jumps in front of the Town Hall, some surfers out on the sea, and children practising for the renowned Kids' R Us Christmas musical extravaganza.

Parents are clearly asking themselves, and other parents, how to create a more family-oriented, child-friendly world, as an alternative to retreating into the privatized worlds of an overly individualistic culture. Parents, alive to the pressures of modern life such as media intrusion, are ensuring that they pay attention to such childhood essentials as loving relationships, conversation, shared mealtimes, stories, reading, rhythmical days, enjoying nature, games, making things, and celebration. Something they are increasingly discovering is that limiting access to the electronic media results in both a calmer, and a more active, fulfilling family life in which children can and do thrive. As Harry, a 19 year old attending a special school said of the family where he lodges 'It's quiet here, and even though we have five TVs at home, it's more fun here because we play games, have meals together and talk.'

Help is also at hand from advocacy organizations like the Alliance for Childhood, which urges both families and schools to provide the essentials for a healthy childhood. They recommend the following childhood essentials, confirmed both by research and by sound common sense:

- Close, loving relationships with responsible adults.
- Outdoor activity, nature exploration, gardening, and other direct encounters with nature.
- Time for unstructured play, especially make-believe play, as part of the core curriculum for young children.
- Music, drama, puppetry, dance, painting, and the other arts, offered both as separate classes and as a kind of 'yeast' to bring the full range of other academic subjects to life.
- Hands-on lessons, handcrafts, and other physically engaging activities, which literally embody the most effective lessons for children in the sciences, mathematics, and technology.
- Conversation, poetry, story-telling, and books read aloud with beloved adults.[3]

Teachers are working to do the best job they can as educators, conscious that they are expected to deal with more and more children with social, learning, and behavioural difficulties. What would help them most is not more technology, but the fulfilment of more basic needs like reduced class sizes, more special-needs teachers, classroom help, more money for books, literacy, building repairs, funding for more arts, craft activities, drama, gardening, cookery, environmental education, sports, and music lessons. A major concern of teachers is that in a public expenditure 'zero-sum game', the large amounts of money spent on buying, maintaining, and staffing ICT are effectively being withdrawn from other important activities like the arts. Many teachers would agree with Steve Jobs, of Apple Computers, who said that,

> 'I've probably spearheaded giving away more computer equipment to schools than anybody on the planet. But I've come to the conclusion that the problem is not one that technology can hope to solve. What's wrong with education cannot be fixed with technology. No amount of technology will make a dent.'[4]

Teachers and parents are also alert to the research agendas of enlightened academics, and draw upon the latest research to justify a more discriminating use of the media. For example, parents the world over are increasingly worried about the effects of the violence seen on TV, videos, and computer games. One recent study by Thomas Robinson at the University of Stanford, California showed that switching off the television significantly reduces levels of child aggression. Some 225 children aged 8 to 9 watched on average 15½ hours per week, as well as five hours of videos and three hours playing video games. One group stopped watching TV for ten days and then limited viewing to only seven hours per week thereafter. This group showed a reduction in violent behaviour of 25 per cent. 'The very good news is that if you help your children to reduce their exposure to media … you'll see a reduction in aggressive behaviour.' He suggested no TV sets or PCs in bedrooms, and that parents together agree a weekly TV and video budget.[5]

Parents who are fed up with the commercial push at Christmas have long blamed TV commercials. And it's now official – the more adverts that children watch, the more Christmas presents they want. In Britain, where children watch on average 18,000 commercials a year, they want many more products than children in Sweden, where TV advertising to children is banned. Researchers at the University of Hertfordshire commented that 'Parents who allow their children to watch a lot of TV in order to give themselves an "easier" life may, in fact, be creating more problems for themselves in the long run.[6]

People in communities are also asking how they can design and maintain family-friendly neighbourhoods, as it takes a whole village to raise a child. One trigger for this is child safety: in Britain, for example, the number of road deaths and accidents sustained by children has declined markedly over the last few years – but only because parents keep their children off the streets or drive them to school. So in Britain, when towns, villages, and neighbourhoods appraise what facilities they have, a recurrent key factor is that of re-designing public spaces with children's needs in mind.

Communities are also connecting violent video games with road deaths as well as violent crime. Jan Wildman is a Gloucester parent whose daughter Cassie was run down by a car driver whilst she was crossing a road. She links such deaths with the violent video game *Carmageddon* and *Grand Auto Theft*, and campaigned vigorously for local shops to stop selling such games.[7] The successor game to *Grand Auto Theft*, *Grand Auto Theft City* for Play Station 2, was the fastest selling title ever in 2002 in Britain, making £10 million in sales soon after its release. This specially violent bestseller carries an 18 year 'X' certificate, even though it was top of the Christmas wish-list for many 10 year olds under peer pressure to get hold of it. Players can take the role of a gangster, Tommy, who cruises around looking for violence, for example running a pizza delivery man off the road and then reversing his car over his body.[8]

Public pressure for the compulsory rating of all video games, with very clear labelling to inform parents, is growing throughout Europe. But there is also a case for censorship and even the banning of such games as *Hooligans, Storm over Europe,* and *Carmageddon,* even though this may be pushing a river. However, the British government's Home Office is still prevaricating on the links between computer violence and increased aggressive behaviour amongst children.[9]

The assertion that the links between media violence and behaviour are unproven is commonly glibly proposed by apologists for media violence – and, of course, by video-games manufacturers. Games like *Doom* or *Quake* plunge the player into a three-dimensional world where you have to kill to survive: ' … few things in life are more exhilarating than spinning around and blowing the thing to kingdom come, the flying gibs so lifelike you can almost feel wet blood'.[10] *Doom* was updated by the US marines for training troops how to kill, so that soldiers played *Doom* to feel like they were in a war situation, where you have one-shot kills. Lt Col. Dave Grossman is citing such examples in the prosecution in the United States of games manufacturers for the Paducah school mass killings by the Kentucky teenager Michael Carneal. The recent hit film, 'Bowling for Columbine' by Michael Moore, explores this theme further.

Unlike the British government, Professor Elizabeth Newson of the University of Nottingham made a strong case for video violence having been a contributory factor in the torture and killing of 2-year-old James Bulger by 10-year-old Jon Venables and Robert Thompson in February 1993. She cited several authoritative studies demonstrating the links, and that there is a vast body of world-wide research of more than 1,000 published papers linking heavy exposure to media violence with aggressive behaviour. She advocated much more research to keep pace with the acceleration of violent content in all its burgeoning interactive forms.

Professor Newson also concludes by saying that the tight regulation of violent media material is needed so as to protect children from potential abuse:

'many of us hold our liberal ideals of freedom of expression dear, but now begin to feel that we were naive in our failure to predict the extent of damaging material and its all too free availability to children. Most of us would prefer to rely on the discretion and responsibility of parents, both in controlling their children's viewing and in giving children clear models of their own distress in witnessing sadistic brutality; however it is unhappily evident that many children cannot rely on their parents in this respect. By restricting such material from home viewing, society must take on a necessary responsibility in protecting children from this as from other forms of child abuse.'[11]

Steve Jobs of Apple Computers argued above that schools' problems cannot be solved by technology alone. Yet the project by politicians, the electronic media, and computer companies to push screen culture into homes and schools continues. The presence of ICT in schools and homes, whilst valuable as a tool, can easily be seen by politicians as a magic silver-bullet solution, a simplistic cure-all, a diversion from the complex work of raising children and providing creative education in the context of a supportive neighbourhood.

However, even in high-tech companies, managers are bemoaning the fact that staff in nearby desks are sending each other e-mails rather than talking – and some are on e-mail for as much as three hours a day. Leading-edge managers thus now see their job as enabling good conversation between people, and staff go on story-telling courses run by story-tellers or actors to improve their communication skills! And so it comes full circle … as the rich, developmentally nourishing diet of play, language development, and social and creative learning in Kindergarten, and in infants and junior schools, is crowded out by the electronic media, then back comes story-telling for high-tech managers and staff because they lack communication skills! As they say now, 'All that I ever learned was in Kindergarten – except these days it's *High-tech-tots-garden!*'

Over and over again, parents and educators in Britain and North America have advocated the abolition of advertising directed at children. For example, Dr Susan Linn of the Judge Baker Children's Centre of the Harvard Medical School writes that,

'With the confluence of sophisticated electronic media technology and the glorification of the free market, it is difficult to
provide children with the kind of environment Winnicott
describes [i.e. good-enough parenting, love, security, and safe
"transitional space" for creativity and growth -ML). American
children are assaulted with the noise from advertising and the
things it sells from the moment they wake up until bedtime.
The space for their own ideas, their own images, their interactions with print or pictures shrinks with every blockbuster, children's film or television programme – inevitably accompanied
by toys, picture books, videos, tapes and clothing.'[12]

Her solution, with colleagues, is a public health campaign to
halt the commercial exploitation of children by eliminating
marketing to children under 8 years of age. The goals of SCEC are
set out in Box 17.

Box 17

Stop the Commercial Exploitation of Children

'Children deserve to grow up free of commercial exploitation!

To protect our children's health and well being, SCEC calls on
national legislators and policy makers to:

- Make schools commercial-free zones;
- Fund research into the psycho-social and health consequences of marketing to children;
- Implement the same federal standards for using children in
academic research;
- Require the Federal Trade Commission to investigate
corporate marketing practices aimed at children;

- Reinstate Federal Communications Commission regulations that prohibit linking TV shows to product promotion;
- Implement uniform age-specific rating standards across all media and 'spin-of' products, including toys and food;
- Eliminate marketing to children under 8 years of age.'

(at www.commercialexploitation.com)

In Europe, Swedish law goes further than what SCEC is proposing by prohibiting TV advertising to children of up to 12 years. Lars Maren of the Swedish Ministry for Culture writes that Swedish law on advertising to children is as follows:

- TV commercials should not have the purpose of attracting the attention of children under 12;
- Persons and characters that play a prominent part in children's programmes should not appear in TV commercials;
- Commercials should not be broadcast during breaks in children's programmes or immediately before or after children's programmes.[13]

Swedish politicians and officials tried unsuccessfully to get the European Union to tighten up advertising aimed at children, proposing that, firstly, TV advertising aimed at minors under 12 should be prohibited, and secondly, that the word 'direct' be deleted from Article 16: 'Television advertising … shall comply with the following criteria – it shall not directly exhort minors to buy a product or service by exploiting their inexperience or credulity'.[14]

The single greatest protection for our children, therefore, would be *to ban all forms of advertising and commercial sponsorship* which are aimed at children of 12 and under, as is currently practised in

Sweden for TV advertising – but extended to all media. This would help put a stop to the commercialization of childhood, through removing a whole swathe of children's TV, video game, and software programmes serving product placement, indirect advertising of the clothes, video, games, junk drinks, and products delivered via blockbusters, and programmes with designer clothes and brands.

Radical, principled action such as this would lay down a protective boundary around childhood culture. At the same time, a special tax on the advertising of soft drinks and junk food could be devoted specifically to social, community, creative, environmental, sports, educational activities, and projects for improving the lives of children. This tax would constitute a sweet, and highly creative revenge on all the pester power unleashed by advertisers on generations of parents via their children.

A main reason for banning advertising directed at children is that it would protect children against commercialism – but there are other powerful reasons too.

First, Stuart Ewen, a New York sociologist and author of *The Public Mind and All Consuming Images*,[15] considers that the electronic media create 'the opportunity to guide people's thoughts and behaviour in an unprecedented manner right into their living rooms. In private spaces throughout the nation the public is now being assembled, its eyes and ears pointing in the same direction.' (Ewen was referring to the 9/11 events and the 'war against terrorism'.) Children should not be subject to such manipulative guidance, until they are able to exercise discrimination and independent judgement as teenagers.[16]

A second reason for banning advertising aimed at children is given by Edward Bernays, the American founder of public relations who, as the nephew of Sigmund Freud, believed that human behaviour was influenced largely by irrational drives and emotions. He defined 'Public Relations' as 'the engineering of consent'. Advertisers have long known that TV is such a persuasive marketing tool that most young children believe product claims. Marketing expert James McNeal describes the powerful effect advertising has on children:

> 'Children under the age of eight believe advertising uncondition-ally, tend to see it as a logical part of programming, and tend not to perceive the selling intent of it. Advertising to children is virtu-ally all emotion and persuasion. Advertisers put to work all the creativity they can muster to create a fantasy environment … with very little regard for useful information expressed in ways children can understand. Advertisers have the ability to convince children to like and desire practically any product, yet this ability is applied mainly to toys and sugared foods … Children should be viewed as superspecial consumers deserving of superspecial treatment by the marketing system. This is necessary for only a short time, while the children are becoming fully qualified consumers, and it will guarantee happier and more effective customers for all marketers for all time.'[17]

Third, and as discussed earlier, Fred and Merrelyn Emery, eminent Australian psychologists, examined the effects of the TV/CRT medium on humans, and concluded that it turned off our brains – unlike for example, reading, which was found to do the opposite. Advertisers know this, of course, so they employ powerful images to plant resonant, positive feelings in us – which are then evoked when we then meet the product on the shelves. Children need protection from this electronic massage.

Fourth, the desire for junk food, currently a major public health threat to children, is implanted via the electronic media.

A fifth argument against child-directed advertising concerns advertisers' aim to deliver children's minds for life, at an age when children are vulnerable, and find it difficult if not impossible to switch off and to resist subtle commercial messages. *Any rational, enlightened society which places children's health and well-being above commercial interests surely has the right to put a stop to this unjustified intrusion into children's lives.*

Sixth, advertisers, unless stopped by law, will go to ever-greater lengths to influence the buying and lifestyle decisions of children. Their aim is to control the life and cultural space of children and teenagers. Naomi Klein recounts, for example, how companies like Nike first pillaged black Ghetto youth culture and then exploited 'coolness' to sell to other teenagers. An advertiser called David Lubars believed that his industry's leading principle was to treat consumers like cockroaches – 'you spray them and spray them and they get immune after a while'. So let's stop them 'spraying' our children and young people with the gimmies! ...[18]

Seventh, whilst the Internet is a huge success in terms of enabling effective communication globally, it is currently being spoilt by a deluge of unsolicited spam, junk e-mail and pornography. The child of a friend innocently did an Internet search for 'woodpeckers' and was immediately bombarded by pornography. Another family kept their internetted computer in the kitchen, so that the parents could monitor its use. This was just as well because when their 9 year old accidentally opened an innocent sounding e-mail the pornographic message then uploaded as the default Home Page! Whilst there are software filters available for pornography and violence there is also a case for the tight regulation, if not banning of violence and pornography pushed on the Internet.

Finally, removing advertising directed at children and adolescents' lives will stop what is a huge cause of stress on families. Parents will be delighted to see the back of advertising-driven pester power! Such a ban could also save a great deal of money for parents, whilst freeing up children's cultural space.

To conclude, then, when parents of young children control the electronic media, they are helping their children to have a childhood. The limiting of media access until older children can read, write well, play by themselves, have sustained interests or hobbies, and make discriminating choices is also important – as the electronic media are, as we have seen, powerfully addictive, and 'steal' huge amounts of time. Schools can also choose to limit electronic media use in the early years when the natural developmental essentials of a vulnerable young childhood are absolutely vital.

However, limiting electronic media access to families and schools is not just a private decision, but also a global political issue. Indonesian parents are just as worried about the impact of media violence and advertising on their children as are British and American families. Globally, a very well-paid army of skilled marketers and psychologists has colonized the cultural space of families, schools, and childhood for private profit. By banning *all* forms of advertising directed at children and young people, we will be able to reclaim childhood from the companies who are branding children for profit.

It is a sad reality of modern corporate life that the only language that marketers and corporations seem to understand, and take notice of, is legislation and coercive regulation. Witness, for example, the frank admission of Bud Konheim, President of Nicole Miller Inc., a clothing company, who has said, 'In this industry, the only reason to change is because someone has got a great big cattle prod that keeps jabbing you in the rear end'.[19] And for those who might doubt the practicality of such a political intervention into the world of big business, we are fortunate to have the Swedish advertising law upon which to build. This banning of advertising directed at children will be the biggest ad-bust and culture jam to date – and it has huge potential to free up children's lives.

However, a tax of, say, 10 per cent on the remaining advertising expenditure could also be exclusively channelled into a charitable Children's Fund, which would disseminate grants to community groups and schools who are enriching children's lives with artistic, sporting, environmental, social, and educational activities. This might at least begin to make up for the negative impact of years of unregulated – and often unprincipled – media manipulation of our children's lives and development. And perhaps most important of all – it would encourage *the reclaiming of childhood* through a veritable explosion of creative, engaging activities from which *all* children could potentially benefit, as this deep and desperately needed cultural transformation has the opportunity to take root and grow.

To conclude, the central message of this book has been that parents *can* make a difference to their children's childhood experience: that we are *not* helpless victims of the corporate media machine and of soulless technological imperatives, and that we can take responsibility for protecting our children from the worst excesses of a toxic screen culture. Neil Postman was undoubtedly saying something similar when he wrote:

'There are parents ... who are defying the directives of their culture. Such parents are not only helping their children to have a childhood ... Those parents ... will help to keep alive a human tradition. [Our culture] is halfway toward forgetting that children need childhood. Those who insist on remembering shall perform a noble service.'[20]

Footnotes and References

Foreword

1 Reported in 'Screen violence is killing us', *Harvard Magazine*, November/December 1993, p. 42.

Chapter 1

1 See http://www.commercialexplotation.com/facts_about_marketing; and *The Lancet*, Vol. 360, No. 9338, 28 September 2002, p. 959.

2 Faith McLellan, 'Marketing and advertising: harmful to children's health', *The Lancet*, ibid., p. 1001.

3 Ibid.

4 See, for example, C. Clouder, S. Jenkinson, and M. Large (eds), *The Future of Childhood*, Hawthorn Press, Stroud, Great Britain, 2000, pp. 91–2.

5 Independent Television Commission, *Television: The Public's View*, London, July 2001.

6 Sonia Livingstone, 'Young people, new media', interviewed by Peter Gliesen, *Interactions*, November-December 1999. See also Sonia Livingstone, Press Release, 27 June 2001, 'UK children are Europe's biggest screen gazers'; and her *Young People and New Media*, Sage, London, 2002. See also http://www.lse.ac.uk/depts/media/people/slivingstone/index.html

7 Ros Coward, 'Room with a view', *Guardian* newspaper, 4 March 1998; Janine Gibson, *Guardian* newspaper, 19 March 1990.

8 Tim Philips, 'King of the classroom', *Guardian* newspaper, 22 January 1998.

9 See, for example, Sally Jenkinson, *The Genius of Play*, Hawthorn Press, Stroud, Great Britain, 2001, p.167.

10 See, for example, www.tvturnoff.org; also, Jenkinson, ibid., pp. 167–9.

11 See, for example, *A Spoonful of Sugar*, Consumers International (24 Highbury Crescent, London N5 1RX), 1997.

12 Jerry Mander, Schumacher Lecture, *Resurgence*, No. 165, 1994.

13 Quoted in *The White Dot* (Brighton, UK), issue 2, April 1998.

Chapter 2

1 Jerry Mander, *Four Arguments for the Elimination of Television*, William Morrow, New York, 1977. See also J. Mander, *In the Absence of the Sacred*, Sierra Book Club, San Francisco, 1991; and www.adbusters.org

2 J. Mander, 'The tyranny of television', Schumacher Lecture, Part II, *Resurgence* magazine, No.165, July-August 1994.

3 See Bernard McGrane's *The Zen TV Experiment* at www.abusters.org

4 See Mander, *Four Arguments for the Elimination of Television*, op. cit., p.159.

5 www.adbusters.org, op. cit.

6 Adapted from 'Screen tests', *New Internationalist* (Oxford, UK), January 1983, pp. 16–17. See also *Let's get Critical: A Media Literacy Toolkit for Parents, Kids and Teachers* at www.mediachannel.org/getinvolved/teachkids.shtml

7 M. Winn, *The Plug-In-Drug*, Bantam Books, New York, 1977.

Chapter 3

1 Both stories told to the author by Russell Evans through personal communication, 2002.

2 David Elkind, *Growing Up Too Fast Too Soon*, Addison-Wesley, Reading, Mass., 1981.

3 Dr Frederic Leboyer, *Birth without Violence*, Wildwood House, London, 1975.

4 R.M. Crosby, *Reading and the Dyslexic Child*, Souvenir Press, London, 1980.

5 Eva Frommer, *Voyage through Childhood into the Adult World*, Hawthorn Press, Stroud, UK, 1986, p. 23.

6 Frommer, *Voyage*, ibid., p. 36.

7 John Gray, *Children are from Heaven*, Vermilion, London, 1999, Chapter 4.

Chapter 4

1 Neil Postman is quoted from a Harvard electronic media conference in Todd Oppenheimer, 'The computer delusion', *Atlantic Monthly*, July 1997, pp. 45–63.

2 See Martin Large, *Who's Bringing Them Up?*, Hawthorn Press, Stroud, Great Britain, 1998, p. 63.

3 Rosie Waterhouse and Colin Brennan, 'Children at risk of mobile phone radiation', *The Sunday Times*, 18 November 2001, p. 19, reporting on the research of Om Gandhi at the University of Utah.

4 See Colleen Cordes and Edward Miller, *Fool's Gold: A Critical Look at Computers in Childhood*, Alliance for Childhood, College Park, Maryland, 2000, p. 39. See also www.allianceforchildhood.net

5 F. Emery and M. Emery, *A Choice of Futures – To Enlighten or Inform*, No. ACP 2600, Centre for Continuing Education, Australian National University (ANU), Canberra, 1975. Merrelyn Emery wrote her doctoral thesis on the maladaptive nature of the CRT for the human brain (M. Emery, 'The Social and Neuropsychological Effects of Television and their Implications for Marketing Practice: An investigation of Adaptation to the CRT', unpublished Ph.D. thesis, ANU, Canberra, 1985).

6 See 'Long-distance hypnosis', *New Internationalist* (Oxford), January 1985, pp. 24–5.

7 Quoted in Joyce Nelson, *The Perfect Machine: TV in the Nuclear Age*, Between the Lines, Toronto, 1987.

8 Nelson, ibid., p. 69.

9 *New Internationalist*, January 1985 (op. cit.), p. 25.

10 Nelson, op. cit., p. 70. See also H. Krugman, *Electroencephalographic Aspects of Low Involvement Implications for the McLuhan Hypothesis*, American Association for Public Opinion Research, 1970.

11 Emery, *A Choice of Futures*, op. cit.

12 Nelson, op. cit., p. 73.

13 K. Buzzell, *The Children of Cyclops*, Association of Waldorf Schools of North America, Fair Oaks, California, 1998; Susan Johnson M.D., 'Strangers in our homes: TV and our children's minds', paper presented at the Waldorf School of San Francisco, 1999.

14 J. Healy, *Endangered Minds: Why Children Don't Think and What We Can Do about It*, Simon & Schuster, New York, 1990.

15 Tim Utton, 'Is life in front of the screen making a spectacle of Britain?', *Daily Mail*, 26th September, 2002, p. 23.

16 Charles Krebs, *A Revolutionary Way of Thinking*, Hill of Content, 1998, emphasis added.

17 Healy, op. cit.

18 On the work of Sally Ward, see Peter Hitchens, 'How TV harms the minds of our children', *Daily Express*, 11 January 1996; Michael Patterson and Janet Boyle, 'Too much TV "delays first words" ', *Scotsman* newspaper, 10 January 1996. In 1996 Dr Sally Ward developed WILSTAAR for language development whilst at the Mancunian Community Health Trust. See also Sally Ward's *Babytalk*, Century, London, 2000 for her babytalk programme.

19 Sarah Bosely, *Guardian* newspaper, 10 January 1996.

20 Peter Hitchens, 'How TV harms … ', op. cit.

21 Patterson and Boyle, op. cit.

22 Audrey E. McAllen, 2002, interview with the author.

23 Willi Aeppli, *The Care and Development of the Human Senses*, Steiner Schools Fellowship Publications, Forest Row, 1993, pp. 22–3. See also A. Soesman, *Our Twelve Senses*, Hawthorn Press, Stroud, Great Britain, 1998.

24 H.D. Levinson, MD, *A Scientific Watergate, Dyslexia*, Stonebridge Publishing Ltd, Lake Success, New York, 1994.

25 See A. Hall, *Water, Electricity and Health*, Hawthorn Press, Stroud, Great Britain, 1996.

26 James Gleick, *Faster: The Acceleration of Just about Everything*, Pantheon Books, New York, 1999.

27 Kim Brooking Payne, *Games Children Play*, Hawthorn Press, Stroud, Great Britain, 1995. See the Foreword by Cheryl Sanders for this discussion.

Chapter 5

1 Frederic Leboyer, *Birth without Violence*, Wildwood House, London, 1975, p. 16.

2 J.N. Ott, *Health and Light*, Pocket Books, New York, 1976.

3 See J. Mander, *Four Arguments for the Elimination of Television*, William Morrow, New York, 1977, pp. 175 and 178.

4 'Those tired children', *Time* magazine, 6 November 1964.

5 Ott, ibid., pp. 125–7.

6 Wurtman, quoted in Mander, op.cit., p. 180.

7 Charles Krebs, *A Revolutionary Way of Thinking*, Hill of Content, 1998, p. 310.

8 Ibid., p. 302.

9 On kinesiology, see Krebs, ibid., and also Appendix 3 for Brain Gym references.

10 US Environmental Protection Agency, *Office Equipment: Design, Indoor Air Emissions and Pollution Prevention Opportunities*, March 1995.

11 See Colleen Cordes and Edward Miller, *Fool's Gold: A Critical Look at Computers in Childhood*, Alliance for Childhood, College Park, Maryland, 2000, p. 21.

12 Cf. www.commercialexploitation.com, SCEC website, Harvard Medical School, Boston.

13 S. Oates, G. Evans, and A. Hedge, 'A preliminary ergonomic and postural assessment of computer work settings in American elementary schools', *Computers in the Schools*, 14 (3–4), 1998, pp. 55–63; and L. Straker, K. Jones, and J. Miller, 'A comparison of the postures assumed when using laptop computers and desktop computers', *Applied Ergonomics*, 28, 1997, pp. 263–8.

14 Phyllis Weikart, *Round the Circle: Key Experiences Movement*, Ypsilanti, MI: High Scope Press, 1986 (emphasis added), quoted in A. Armstrong and C. Casement, *The Child and the Machine*, Key Porter Books, Toronto, Canada, 1998, p. 63.

15 Carla Hannaford, *Smart Moves*, Great Ocean, NC, 1995, p. 97.

16 From an interview with Aonghus Gordon.

Chapter 6

1 D. Burke and J. Lotus, *Get a Life! The Little Red Book of the Anti-Television Campaign*, Bloomsbury, London, 1996, pp. 189–90.

2 Robert D. Puttnam, 'Tuning in, tuning out: the strange disappearance of social capital in America', The 1995 Ithiel de Soal Pool Lecture, *Political Science and Politics*, 28 (4), December 1995.

3 Sally Jenkinson, *The Genius of Play*, Hawthorn Press, Stroud, Great Britain, 2001, p. 163.

4 Robert Kubey and Mihaly Csikszentmihalyi, 'Television addiction is no mere metaphor', *Scientific American*, February 2002, pp. 62–8.

5 James Meikle, 'Computer boy gets miner's white finger', *Guardian* newspaper, 1 February 2002.

6 Jenkinson, *The Genius of Play*, op. cit., p. 97.

7 Tannis Macbeth Williams, *The Impact of Television*, Academic Press, Orlando, Florida, 1986.

8 Diane E. Levin, 'Media, culture and the undermining of play in the United States', in E. Klugman (ed.), *Play, Policy and Practice*, Redleaf Press, St Paul, Minnesota, 1995, pp. 177–8.

9 Williams, op. cit.

10 Tim Hicks, unpublished paper, Sebastopol, Calif.

11 Jane Healy, *Failure to Connect: How Computers Affect Our Children's Minds – for Better and Worse*, Simon & Schuster, New York, 1998, p. 64.

12 M. Messenger Davis, *Television is Good for Your Kids*, Hilary Shipman, London, 1993, p. 192.

13 Committee on Communications, American Academy of Pediatrics, Policy Statement: 'Children, Adolescents, and Advertising' (RE9504), Chicago, American Academy of Pediatrics, 1995. Also, G. Stewart, 'Doctors declare war on child ads', *Evening Standard*, 12 November 1988, p. 12.

14 David Piachaud, 'Present dangers', *Guardian* newspaper, 19 December 2002.

15 D. Singer and J. Singer, 'Some hazards of growing up in a television environment: children's aggression and restlessness', in S. Oskamp (ed.), *Television as a Social Issue*, Sage, London, 1988, p. 185.

16 See Jenkinson, *The Genius of Play*, op. cit. Figures compiled by TV-Free America, Connecticut Avenue, NW Suite 3A, Washington, DC 20009

17 B. Centerwell, 'Television and violence', *Journal of the American Medical Association*, 267, 1992, pp. 3059–63.

18 Quoted in Jenkinson, *The Genius of Play*, op. cit., p 162.

19 Williams, op. cit.

20 W.A. Belson, *Television Violence and the Adolescent Boy*, Saxon House, London, 1982.

21 Williams, op. cit.

22 Professor Tony Charlton and his research colleagues at the University of Gloucestershire, Cheltenham, conducted a range of research projects on the introduction of satellite TV into St Helena.

23 David Grossman, 'Teaching kids to kill', in C. Clouder, S. Jenkinson, and M. Large (eds), *The Future of Childhood*, Hawthorn Press, Stroud, Great Britain, 2000, pp. 142–3.

24 Centerwell, op. cit.

25 Grossman, 'Teaching kids to kill', op. cit, pp. 144–5.

26 Burke and Lotus, op. cit., pp. 179–83.

27 Jeffrey Johnson, Patricia Cohen, Elizabeth Smailes, Stephanie Kasen, and Judith S. Brook, 'Television viewing and aggressive behavior during adolescence and adulthood', *Science*, January 2002; contact jjohnson@pi.cpmc.columbia.edu

28 Personal e-mail communication to the author, November 2002.

29 References in this section are variously drawn from the following sources: D. Grossman, 'Teaching kids to kill', in C. Clouder, S. Jenkinson and M. Large (eds), *The Future of Childhood*, Hawthorn Press, Stroud, Great Britain, 2000; D. Grossman, *Stop Teaching our Kids to Kill: A Call to Action Against TV, Movie and Video Game Violence*, Random House, New York, 1999.

Chapter 7

1   Todd Oppenheimer, 'The computer delusion', *Atlantic Monthly*, July 1997.

2   David Roberts and Richard House, 'Toys aren't us' (Letters), *The Independent* newspaper Education Supplement, 18 November 1999, p. 6.

3   C. Stoll, *High Tech Heretic*, Doubleday, New York, 1999.

4   John Ezard, 'TV puts paid to the nursery rhyme', *Guardian*, 11 May 1978.

5   Harry F. Waters, 'What TV does to kids', *Newsweek*, 21 February 1977.

6   Richard DeGrandpre, *Ritalin Nation*, Norton, New York, 2000, p. 158.

7   D. Burke and J. Lotus, *Get a Life! The Little Red Book of the Anti-Television Campaign*, Bloomsbury, London, 1996, pp. 114–15.

8   Richard House, 'Beyond the medicalisation of "challenging behaviour"; or protecting our children from "Pervasive Labelling Disorder" ', *The Mother* magazine, nos 4–6, 2002–3 (published in three parts).

9   Jane Healy, *Endangered Minds: Why Children Don't Think and What We Can Do about It*, Touchstone/Simon & Schuster, New York, 1990.

10 Colleen Cordes and Edward Miller, *Fool's Gold: A Critical Look at Computers in Childhood*, Alliance for Childhood, College Park, Maryland, 2000, p. 37.

11 Jane Healy, *Failure to Connect: How Computers Affect Our Children's Minds – for Better and Worse*, Simon & Schuster, New York, 1998.

12 Sally Goddard Blythe, 'In praise of song and dance', *Times Educational Supplement*, 23 January 1998; 'Music matters', *Music Teacher*, September 1998, p. 43. See also her forthcoming book for the Hawthorn Press 'Early Years' series, *The Well-Balanced Child*, 2004 (in preparation).

13 Sally Jenkinson, *The Genius of Play*, Hawthorn Press, Stroud, Great Britain, 2001.

14 Healy, *Endangered Minds*, op. cit., p. 216.

Chapter 8

1   Ian Murray and Damian Whitworth, 'Older children should be limited to two hours viewing a day', *The Times*, 5 September 1999.

2   E-mail from Dave Grossman to the author, 9 January 2003.

3   *The Times*, Editorial, 5 September 1999.

4   Mary Braid, 'From Pokemon to Plato', *The Independent* newspaper, 2 April 2002.

5   Cathy Drysdale, producer, BBC Radio 4 'Word of Mouth', notes of interview with Dr Sally Ward, 2 August 1996.

6   Dorothy Cohen, 'Is TV a pied piper?', *Young Children Journal*, November 1974, pp. 12–13.

7 'What it feels like to be a girl', *Guardian Weekend* magazine, 16 November 2002; Lauren Greenfield, *Fast Forward: Growing up in the Shadow of Hollywood and Girl Culture*, Chronicle Books, 2002.

8 Jane Healy, *Endangered Minds*, op. cit., and *Failure to Connect*, Simon & Schuster, New York, 1998; personal e-communication to the author, 26 November 2002.

9 Thomas Poplawski, 'Taming the media monster', *Renewal*, Vol. 10, No. 1, Spring/Summer 2001 (Fair Oaks, Sacramento, Calif.).

Chapter 9

1 John Harlow, 'Cruise joins crusade to turn children off TV', *The Sunday Times*, 29 September 2002, p. 28.

2 D. Burke and J. Lotus, *Get a Life! The Little Red Book of the Anti-Television Campaign*, Bloomsbury, London, 1996.

3 Sally Jenkinson, *The Genius of Play*, Hawthorn Press, Stroud, Great Britain, 2001.

4 Stephanie Cooper, Christine Fynes-Clinton, and Marije Rowling, *The Children's Year: Crafts and Clothes for Children and Parents to Make*, Hawthorn Press, Stroud, Great Britain, 1986.

5 Kim Brooking Payne, *Games Children Play*, Hawthorn Press, Stroud, Great Britain, 1996.

6 Diana Carey and Judy Large, *Festivals, Family,* and *Food,* Hawthorn Press, Stroud, Great Britain, 1982.

Chapter 10

1 Sarah Cassidy, 'Reading at home', *The Independent*, 20 November 2002, p. 9.

2 There are many books and sources of information on using computers – e.g. J.A. McClellan, *Parents' Guide to the Internet*, Atlantic Books, London, 2001. Chapter 5 deals with protecting your child online.

3 Jim Trelease, *The Read Aloud Handbook*, Penguin, Harmondsworth, 1994.

4 Neil Postman, *The Disappearance of Childhood*, Delacorte Press, New York, 1982, p. 153.

5 From his *Charlie and the Chocolate Factory*, Penguin, Harmondsworth, 1964.

Chapter 11

1 Matt Wells, 'Repeat showings', *Guardian*, 15 November 2001.

2 Nicci Gerrard, 'What's worrying our kids?', *Observer*, 14 February 1999.

3 Colleen Cordes and Edward Miller, *Fool's Gold: A Critical look at Computers in Childhood*, Alliance for Childhood, College Park, Maryland, p. 47.

4 Steve Jobs, *Wired Magazine*, February 1996.

5 Ben MacIntyre, 'Switching off TV cuts childhood aggression', *The Times*, 16 January 2001.

6 J. Chapman, 'Santa's extra long list', *Daily Mail*, 8 November 2002.

7 H. Blow and G. Henderson, 'Time to act over screen violence?', *The Citizen*, 16 December 1997.

8 M. Nixon, 'Boycott this sick Christmas game', *The Mail on Sunday*, 8 December 2002.

9 K. Ahmad, 'Age limits for children on violent video games', *Observer*, 29 December 2002.

10 P. Keegan, 'In the line of fire', *Guardian*, 1 June 1999.

11 E. Newson, 'Video violence and the protection of children', *The Psychologist*, June 1994.

12 S. Linn, 'J.K. Rowling and the Golden Calf: Harry Potter Inc. is about to mesmerise the market place', *Boston Globe*, 9 July 2000.

13 E-mail to author, 20 December 2002, from Lars Maren, Ministry of Culture, Sweden. See also 'Television without Frontiers Directive' at www.europa.eu.int/ institutions/commission/audiovisualpolicy/regulatory   framework/television and cinema; and the report by Gunilla Jarlbro and Ehrling Bjurstrom at www.konsumentverket.se/In English /Books and booklets).

14 Lars Maren, ibid.: www.europa.eu.int/institutions/commission/audiovi-sual/studies and reports/Study of the impact of television advertising and tele-hopping on minors.

15 Stuart Ewen, *The Public Mind and All Consuming Images*, New York. See also Stuart Ewen and Elizabeth Ewan, *Chambers of Desire: Mass Images and the Shaping of American Consciousness*, New York, 1992.

16 Julia Hobsbawm, 'How they all took us hostage', *Observer*, 16 November 2001.

17 David Piachaud, 'Present Danger', *Guardian*, 19 December 1999.

18 Naomi Klein, *No Logo*, HarperCollins, London, 2001, p.9.

19 Ibid., p. 423.

20 Neil Postman, *The Disappearance of Childhood*, Vintage Books, New York, 1994.

Bibliography

Alliance for Childhood (2000) *Fool's Gold: A Critical Look at Computers in Child-hood*, College Park, Maryland, USA

Armstrong, A., and Casement, C. (1998) *The Child and the Machine: Why Computers May Put Our Children's Education at Risk,* Key Porter Books, Toronto

Biddulph, S. (1998) *The Secret of Happy Children,* HarperCollins, London

Burke, D., and Lotus, J. (1998) *Get a Life,* Bloomsbury, London

Buzzell, K. (1998) *The Children of Cyclops: The Influence of Television Viewing on the Developing Human Brain,* Association of Waldorf Schools of North America, Fair Oaks, Calif.

Carlsson-Paige N., and Levin D.I. (1990) *Who's Calling the Shots? How to Respond Effectively to Children's Fascination with War Play and War Toys and Violent TV,* New Society Publishers, Gabriola Island, Vancouver

Chilton Pearce, J. (1992) *Evolution's End: Claiming the Potential of Our Intelligence,* HarperCollins, San Francisco

DeGrandpre, R. (2000) *Ritalin Nation: Rapid-Fire Culture and the Transforma-tion of Human Consciousness,* W. W. Norton, New York

Elkind, D. (1981) *The Hurried Child: Growing Up Too Fast Too Soon,* Addison-Wesley, Reading, Mass.

Elkind, D. (1987) *Mis-education: Pre-schoolers at Risk,* A.A. Knopf, New York

Evans, R. (2000) *Helping Children to Overcome Fear: The Healing Power of Play,* Hawthorn Press, Stroud

Healy, J.M. (1990) *Endangered Minds: Why Children Don't Think and What We Can Do about It,* Touchstone/Simon & Schuster, New York

Healy, J.M. (1998) *Failure to Connect: How Computers Affect Our Children's Minds – for Better and Worse,* Simon & Schuster, New York

Herman, E.S., and Chomsky, N. (1988) *Manufacturing Consent: The Political Economy of the Mass Media*, Pantheon, London

Jenkinson, S. (2001) *The Genius of Play: Celebrating the Spirit of Childhood*, Hawthorn Press, Stroud

Klein, N. (2001) *No Logo,* HarperCollins, Flamingo, London

Livingstone, S. (2002) *Young People and New Media*, Sage, London

McClellan, J. (2001) *A Parent's Guide to the Internet*, The Guardian, Atlantic Books, London

Mander, J. (1977) *Four Arguments for the Elimination of Television*, Quill, New York

Mander, J. (1992) *In the Absence of the Sacred,* Sierra Book Club, San Francisco

Medved, M. & Medved, D. (1998) *Saving Childhood: Protecting Our Children from the National Assault on Innocence*, HarperCollins, Zondervan

Postman, N. (1994) *The Disappearance of Childhood,* Vintage Books, New York

Roszak, T. (1995) *The Cult of Information: A Neo-Luddite Treatise on High Tech,* University of California Press, San Francisco

Sanders, B. (1995) *A is for Ox: The Collapse of Literacy and the Rise of Violence in an Electronic Age*, Vintage Books, New York

Setzer, W. (1989) *Computers in Education*, Floris, Edinburgh

Stoll, C. (1995) *Silicon Snake Oil,* Doubleday, New York

Winn, M. (1985) *The Plug-in Drug*, Penguin, New York and London

Michael Moore's 2002 film, *Bowling for Columbine,* is very relevant to the issue of violence and the media, and makes an excellent discussion springboard. He explores the 20th April 1999 shooting of 13 students and one teacher by two students at Columbine School, Littleton, Colorado, against the context of US gun culture.

Resources

American Academy of Pediatrics

www.aap.org/family/mediaimpact

Alliance for Childhood

The Alliance for Childhood is a forum for partnerships of individuals or organizations who work together out of respect for childhood in a world-wide effort to improve children's lives.

- *USA*: PO Box 444, College Park, MD 20741 (01)301 699 9058 www.alliance for childhood.org
- *Britain*: www.allianceforchildhood.org.uk or via www.steinerwaldorf.org.uk

Centre for Media Literacy

www.medialit.org

ICT Curriculum Resources in Steiner/Waldorf Education

For the development of age appropriate, *Information and Communication Technology Curriculum for Steiner Waldorf Schools*, contact Ewout

Van Manen, Michael Hall Rudolf Steiner School, Forest Row, East Sussex, RH18 5JA, Britain evm@michaelhall.co.uk

Media Foundation

adbusters@adbusters.org   www.adbusters.org

Projects include Adbusters Magazine and Culture Jammers Headquarters Website.

1243 West 7th Avenue, Vancouver, BC, V6H 1B7, Canada
Tel +1 604 736 9401

Media Channel

'As the media watch the world, we watch the media'.

1600 Broadway, Suite 700, New York, NY 10019, USA

www.mediachannel.org

Stop Commercial Exploitation of Children

SCEC's website is: www.commercialexploitation.com

Dr Susan Linn of the Judge Baker Children's Centre at the Harvard Medical School is writing a new book for 2003 provisionally called *Shared Minds: What Corporations Want from Our Children*

TV Turn-off Week: TV Turn-off Network

Usually in the last full week of April each year.

White Dot, PO Box 2116, Hove, East Sussex, BN3 3LR Britain
PO Box 577257, Chicago, Ill., 60657 USA
www.tvturnoff.org   www.whitedot.org
(Was TV Free America)

Appendix 1

Protecting Children on the Internet

The hazards of online pornography, stranger danger in chat rooms, violence and other unsuitable content have been much discussed. However, taking sensible precautions like having the internetted computer in a shared family space such as the kitchen or hall-way where you can supervise use is a good start. Understanding how the Internet works, and a review of the potential risks is a big help as well.

Risks to your children include the following:

- Chat rooms and Usenet newsgroups can be risky, for example with 'cyber predators' stalking or grooming a child so as to trick them into meeting in real life. Cyber stalkers can harass children online with threats of viruses and frightening e-mails, and hacking into their computers.
- Your child could access information such as porn, violent images, gore, hate/racist material, conspiracy theories, misinformation that is dangerous, disturbing and inappropriate.
- Children can give away private information about themselves that can be used for marketing and by cyber stalkers.
- Your credit card details, if they can get hold of them, can be used to buy illegal goods.

Children can also cause damage and risks to others. There have been cases of online bullying and cyber stalking by children, of other children, online. The family computer may be infected with viruses, because unknown e-mails have been opened or risky sites visited. They might shop online with your credit card, or hack illegally into others' computers.

The risks can be easily reduced by simple methods including:

1. Locate the family computer in a social space where you can keep an eye on use.

   • Avoid using your work internet account at home, forbid your children to protect areas of the computer with a password, learn how the computer works and avoid leaving any important personal information such as computer passwords, or credit carts around, or in a computer file. Avoid allowing online computers in children's and teenagers' bedrooms.

2. Agree guidelines for Internet use at home

   • How much time per day or week do you want your children to use the computer and be online? What can they access? How can you set and agree ground rules for use? E.g.
     • Daily time budget for being online
     • What is needed for homework?
     • No computer use until homework done
     • Agree ground rules with other parents for use when your child is visiting friends
     • Agree the kinds of websites your child is allowed to visit, and the reasons for certain types of site being off limits,and that your child is free to discuss with you what happened if they access disturbing material accidentally

- Discuss the chat rooms your child can use and check out the discussions that take place in the chat room. (See www.smartparent.org and www.chatdanger.com for more information)

- Agree ground rules that must not be broken. Jim McClellan in, *A Parents Guide to the Internet,* suggests five. (Atlantic Books, Guardian, London, 2001, p 251):

'Five rules for kids

1. Never give out personal/private information without your parents' permission.
2. Never give out your account password to someone who contacts you while you're online claiming to be from your ISP. It doesn't matter how official they sound. A genuine employee/official from your IPS/online service will never ask for information online.
3. Never meet an online friend in the real world unless your mum or dad or another adult you can trust is present.
4. Never reply to threatening/nasty e-mails or chat messages. Instead, save them, and then show them to your mum and dad or another adult who can report them to your mum or dad or another adult who can report them to the relevant authorities.
5. Tell someone if you encounter anyone or anything online that upsets or scares you.'

I personally add a sixth – I normally never open an unsolicited e-mail or attachment unless I know who it is from, because of the danger of Spam, junk mail, viruses, cookies, commercial intrusion, pornography. It also helps to use an ISP that screens out Spam if you can find one!

Discuss these rules with your child so they know this increases safety, and why the ground rules are vital. You can even sign an internet family pledge with your child.

These are the basics for safety on the Internet, through surfing together, teaching your child net literacy is important, for example being critical about commercialism/free offers, being cautious about who they meet online, observing ground rules for chat room discussions, and thinking twice before pressing the SEND button. There are other things beyond the scope of this book to consider such as Internet filtering software. More importantly, books like Jim McClellan's, *Parents' Guide to the Internet* gives lots of useful tips about making the most of the Internet as a resource in the British context. For North America, try, *The Parent's Guide to Protecting Your Children in Cyberspace*, Parry Aftab, McGraw Hill. This also gives Internet child safety information.

Appendix 2

Campaign to Ban Advertising to Children

The British, American and European Advertising industry are, not surprisingly given where their profits come from, very worried about the growing movement amongst parents, educators, doctors and politicians to restrict advertising to children. They are less concerned about the well-being of children, than the threat to banning advertising to children. So the advertisers are actively lobbying and campaigning against any further restriction on advertising.

So our politicians need our help to counter such well-funded lobbying. For example, in Britain, Deborah Shipley M.P. has got the signatures of over 100 M.P.'s for her Early Day Motion to Parliament banning advertising to under fives. There is a EU wide movement by politicians to apply a Europe wide ban. The revising of the *EU Television without Frontiers Directive* between 2002–4 could contain restrictions and mechanisms for introducing a ban, if the public press their national and European politicians to actively support this against the advertising industry's lobbying.

At the same time as the campaign for banning TV advertising to children under twelve, other bans are being discussed such as one on advertising products that appeal to children, stopping the use of brand characters, using children to advertise any product, advertising on radio or in the cinema, sponsorship material in schools and advertising to children on mobile phones and the Internet.

There are widespread precedents to build on for further restricting advertising to children. In Europe, Sweden has banned advertising to children under twelve, with no advertising on children's programmes, though satellite TV from Britain brings commercials. The Swedish Minister for Culture wants children to be declared a 'commercial free zone'. Greece bans the advertising of toys on TV, and is discussing banning advertising to children under 18. Belgium has banned advertising to children, firstly in the Flemish half and now in the French half of the country. Denmark bans advertising five minutes before and after children's programmes. Ireland, with strict self-censorship, bans all advertisements during children's programmes. Italy bans advertising during cartoon programming and has a twenty-minute minimum break between commercials. Poland bans all TV and radio marketing to children, and Norway also bans advertising to children on TV.

ISBA, the voice of British advertisers, 'takes the threat to advertising and children very seriously'. (ISBA Briefing Paper, May 2002, *Advertising to Children* by Joe Lamb) Presumably then, Joe Lamb of ISBA thinks that banning advertising to children is a threat to children? It is certainly a threat to the advertising industry, and ISBA makes a case for countering the restriction or banning of advertising to children based on three major points. Firstly, 'From an early age, children understand the role of advertising. They have a right to access to information and should not be artificially cut off from what is an important part of modern life.'

Joe Lamb, however, was unable to answer my specific question to him, 'At what age do children understand the role of advertising?' He admitted that in fact he was personally no expert on the right age. He writes that children have a right to access to information, but neglects to spell out the difference between neutrally presented information, and commercials with a persuasive intent. What does he mean by his assertion that children should, ' ... not be artificially cut off from what is an important part of modern life'?

If society decides to regulate advertising, for example by banning billboards from the roadside or smoking advertising, what is artificial/wrong with that? And advertising may be 'an important part of modern life' for advertisers, but who judges what is important for children? Surely children have the right to a commercial free life? His second point states that, 'Advertisers respect children. Across the EU existing laws and self-regulatory codes already afford the protection that we as a society expect for our children. This has been endorsed by an EU-commissioned report.'

Advertisers certainly respect children as products, as consumers, but it is debatable whether they respect the right to childhood. They aim to influence children and parents' purchasing decisions through a highly complex mix of advertising via TV, the print media, viral marketing, manipulating peer group pressure, point of sale material, videos, blockbusters, mobile phones and the Internet. According to the director of Saatchi and Saatchi Interactive, the Internet, ' ... is a medium for advertisers that is unprecedented ... there's probably no other product or service that we can think of that is like it in terms of capturing kids' interest ... ' The Saatchi and Saatchi's Kid Connection service claims that:'We at Kid Connection are committed to understanding kids: their motivations, their feelings, and their influences. In keeping with our mission to connect our clients to the kid market with programs that match our clients' business objectives with the needs, drives and desires of kids ... Interactive technology is at the forefront of kid culture, allowing us to enter into contemporary life and communicate with them in an environment they call their own.' (Quoted from Centre for Media Education, 'Web of Deception: Threats to Children from Online Marketing, www.cme.org'. The second Saatchi quote is reproduced from *Marketing to Children*, Sharon Beder http://www.uow.edu.au/arts/sts/sbeder/children.html)

Saatchi and Saatchi are not alone in 'respecting' children, as advertisers to children use anthropologists and psychologists who specialise in 'psycho cultural youth research' to analyse how children use the Internet, react to images, and find out what matters to them. Nintendo in the US interviews 1500 children each week.

Joe Lamb claims not only that advertisers 'respect' children, but that existing EU laws and advertisers' self regulation is fine, and that an EU-commissioned report endorses the current regulatory system. He does not mention that the law firm Bird and Bird's report for the EU did not examine the whole impact of commercials on children, as the Swedish Culture Ministry amongst others had originally wanted, but the limiting of the terms of reference of the Bird regulation report was the result of fierce commercial lobbying.

Thirdly, Joe Lamb claims that the restriction on TV advertising to children would 'inevitably result in the impoverishment of the quality and quantity of children's TV.'

However, this last point flies in the face of BBC TV children's programmes, which have long been commercial free. (www.isba.org.uk)

ISBA is actively countering the threat of banning or restricting advertising through the Advertising Education Forum in Europe (www.aeforum.org) and supports the Children's Programme of the Food Advertising Unit (www.fau.org.uk). The latter is trying to counter the public perception of the links between TV fast food and soft drink commercials and childhood obesity, arguing that many factors other that TV commercials are involved in rising levels of obesity. (Just as they argue that smoking advertising may be a factor in increased smoking and cancer.) ISBA, and some sweet manufacturers, are also supporting Media Smart, the media literacy programme that aims to educate children about advertising.

ISBA members have a total spend on marketing communications of nearly £10 billion p.a., so have huge vested interests in advertising to children. So it's up to parents, educators, health professionals, child psychologists, doctors, and also those individual advertisers who are unhappy with the commercial Adcult they are immersing children in, to lobby for restricting advertising to children. This can be done by meeting national and European politicians personally, public meetings, boycotts of particular offending companies and by letters to your MP and MEP – for a ban on all forms of advertising aimed at children of twelve and under. Another step is to use shareholder power to force companies to introduce ethical advertising policies, which respect childhood as a commercial free zone.

Appendix 3

Movement, Health and Ergonomic Tips for Computer Use

Western life and workstyles are increasingly sedentary, with the resulting health hazards. As increasing use is made of the electronic media, much more research is needed into the health effects, and the research taken out of specialised compartments and seen as a whole.

Doctors, osteopaths, optometrists, chiropractors and other health practitioners are seeing a rise of complaints from adults and children with back pain, poor posture, eyesight problems and movement difficulties. However, help is also at hand with the rise of a whole range of sports, eastern martial arts, artistic and therapeutic movement routines to choose from. Examples include Eastern movement disciplines like Yoga, Tai Chi, Aikido, Judo or Western approaches such as the Alexander Technique, Pilates, Spatial Dynamics (Bothmer Gymnastics), Aerobics, Eurythmy, to mention just a few. There is a lot to choose from, and movement courses are often run by local adult education centres, surgeries or complementary health centres.

Many people take some time out first thing in the morning, or during the day to carry out their preferred exercise routine as a regular part of their day, and such exercise routines have been recommended by health practitioners as preventative or even curative measures for patients. So if in doubt, ask them what they recommend, and you can take advantage of the regular check ups offered by osteopaths, chiropractors or by optometrists, to name a few of the professions involved.

Noticing How the Electronic Media Affect You

I consulted my chiropractor, David Hubbard for his advice, and we worked out together three practical steps people can follow to take more care of their health when using the electronic media: firstly, ask yourself, 'What do you notice when using the electronic media?' Secondly, inform yourself about possible steps to take; thirdly, take practical action and notice the changes.

What do you notice about yourself and others when using the electronic media?

Observations from different people include, 'TV and computers suck my attention in', 'stops conversation', 'makes me drowsy', 'can send me to sleep', 'makes me tense', 'I can't switch off', 'My eyes are dry, vision is blurry', 'I cannot recall what I saw or heard on the program/ computer', 'I can't stop, even though people are calling me for supper', 'I don't know where the time went, I just started surfing on the net and an hour went by just like that'.

Such observations are common, we all know we react in these ways, but it's important as the first step to notice the effects the screen has on you, and how it affects everyone differently. It is a very personal process.

There are broadly three ways the screen can unsynchronize your brain. Firstly, there are the effects on Laterality, on the Left/Right dimension of the body and brain. Your spelling starts going, you lose the ability to think coherently and clearly, your inner dialogue breaks up, it becomes harder to evaluate.

One helpful approach for such symptoms can be Brain Gym, and the 'Midline Movements', one of which is 'Cross Crawl'(see G

& P Dennison, The Brain Gym, Teachers' Edition). Cross lateral activities can help reintegrate the brain function, by moving your body in a synchronized way separate disconnected functions can interrelate to create a more meaningful whole.

Another of the activities is 'Lazy 8s', this encourages a development of hand/eye co-ordination, while at the same time using both hemispheres in the activity.

Secondly, you can lose synchronicity of your brain's cognitive functions either overfocusing or underfocusing. This response is linked to the reptilian brain and the fight, flight and freeze response to threat. In the underfocus mode, your brain switches off, you cannot pay attention, you are in a state of distraction, you are just not absorbed by anything, you cannot connect.

In the opposite focus mode, you are completely absorbed into the screen, you are unable to move away, you cannot switch off, it sucks you in, you are caught, your brain's frontal lobe is knocked out, and you cannot get away from the screen!

The physical effects of the under/over focus is a tension in the front or back muscles of the body or both. This can lead to symptoms including tight neck, tense shoulders, stiff lower back, tight calves and ankles, migraines, RSI (repetitive strain injury).

What helps with the overfocus/underfocus states are 'Lengthening Activities' – these movements help to counterbalance the muscular effects of the 'survival mode'. By gently activating some of the involved muscles the body can bring itself back from the automatic reaction to threat to a more appropriate balanced response. An example exercise is the 'Gravity Glider' which helps to re-establish pelvic and spinal stability and thus position the body in a balanced responsive way (see The Brain Gym).

A third set of reactions is the disconnect mode, which is when you feel that, 'I'm sitting here, and I know I mean to do something else.' 'I have spent hours surfing … what did I do and where did the time go?' 'I am not going to dinner ... just yet!' 'Even though I don't need to be here, I just don't have any will to get out!'

In this kind of disconnect mode you can logically know what to do but be unable to apply the will to do it. Another kind of disconnect response is that of the technophobe, who feels so strongly against using the screen that they won't use computers whatever.

The Brain Gym activities here are the 'Energy Exercises', they stimulate the top/bottom flow in the body brain between the 'feeling' mid-brain and the 'rational' cortex.

Water is a very simple activity in this group. We are dependent on water, it is vital for our health and well-being yet many people are dehydrated and therefore under functioning mentally and perhaps physically ill. Because the body is an adaptive organism if we are chronically dehydrated the body system stops giving thirst indicators which we respond to, therefore we often respond with 'I'm hungry' or 'I'm not thirsty' or 'I don't like water'. A small regular intake of plain water is what we need.

Another activity in this group is 'Brain Buttons' these points when rubbed stimulate circulation to the brain and increase electrical activity between the two hemispheres.

Back in the Office and the Home: Ergonomics

Whilst it is important to check out with the appropriate health professionals about things like back pain, posture and eyesight, -the following brief overview is offered as a starter for work and home physical arrangements for using computers.

Designing your office and home computer workstation is important for your health, and ergonomics as the science of how we as people fit with our tools can help healthy design, so you can find the best fit. We are all different, and ergonomics is vital because back pain is the biggest cause of prolonged time off sick at work: lost days from back pain are rising. When looking at computer work/home station design for you, and also your child, the following things need considering:

1. Seat design: the height of the seat must not be greater than your knee height; knees slightly lower than hips. Seat depth should be no greater than buttock to knee distance. No sliding upholstery, and ensure seat angles of 100–110 degrees. The feet should be comfortably flat on the floor, or on a foot rest. The higher the backrest, the better the support. Chair should be able to tilt 5 degrees, movable with castors and rotatable, easily controlled from sitting position and armrests and give arm and wrist support.

2. The office desk: middle row of keys in line with user's elbow; for writing, desk should be about 2 inches or 50mm above user's elbow height; good leg room between thighs and desk; some people like a pullout keyboard below the desk level.

3. The screen-CRT's have glare, flicker and fluorescent effects-flat screen or liquid crystal screen are much kinder, have less glare/glow and fluorescent effect.

   Screen should be a comfortable size, reasonable brightness and contrast, no flicker, position to avoid glare, top of screen either at eye level, or even better at the same height as the top of your head, to save you looking down/stooping; located in front of user, and minimum viewing distance 500 mm or approx. 18 inches.

   Screens ideally should not be against a wall, because it's not possible then to look into the distance and refocus your vision. You need this distance focus potential because the screen fixes your sight into two dimensions. There is no ocular adjustment for distance, which leads to eye muscle fatigue and ocular lock. You can tell this by the fixed stare on peoples faces, you ask them a question, they then pull back, shake themselves a bit and say,

'What did you say?' It can be helpful to look out of a window over or beside the screen, or have a landscape picture with a horizon to look at.

Laptops require you to look down. Too much of this can be a hazard, so having a separate screen/monitor can help here.

4. The keyboard needs to be the right height for users, usually elbow height, tilted forward by 10–15 degrees, with a good display contrast and responsive keys.

5. Mouse-finger pads on the keyboard can be better than a mouse. The mouse needs to be responsive to movement and click easily, you need to avoid over stretching, and use the mouse mat. Your wrists may need a mouse support if you use a mouse a lot, such as rests and armrests, otherwise the arm muscles can become taut, try then the 'dead mouse', turn your arm and hand over and release the tension.

6. Software should be user friendly, consistent, with training, and with clear commands.

7. With the work environment pay attention to background glare, air quality, room temperature, rest breaks such as at least 5 minutes rest per hour and good lighting levels.

Finally, pay attention to your body's needs and for enough water, and when in doubt consult with a health professional who can work out what's best for you personally – the above guidelines are a general checklist only.

David Hubbard, MMCA, International Faculty Trainer for Educational Kinesiology, McTimoney Chiropractor and Richard Brown DC, MCC, MergS, *Back in the Office*, The Lansdown Clinic, Stroud, Gloucestershire

References

Batmanghelidj, Dr F. (1992 and 2000) *The Body's Many Cries for Water*, Tagman Press

Dennison, G. and P. (1986) *The Brain Gym, Teachers' Edition*, USA

Hannaford, C. (1995) *Smart Moves*, Great Ocean, NC

Ergonomics Society, UK www.ergonomics.org.uk

General Chiropractic Council 0845 601 1796 www.gcc-uk.org

Appendix 4

Holistic Learning in Early Childhood: The Hawthorn Press 'Early Years' Series

Introduction: The Dismembering of Childhood

Founded around the turn of the millennium, the books in this pioneering 'Early Years' series – to which the present book is the latest addition – are providing much-needed nourishment and inspiration in the face of modern culture's crude 'managerial' ethos of over-active, prematurely intellectual intrusion into the very *being* of young children. Since the mid-1990s, a 'formal-schooling' ideology has encroached ever more insidiously into the early years sphere – with the relentless bureaucratization of early learning environments stemming from, for example, tick-box developmental assessments and the imposition of a 'curriculum' on to children as young as 3.

In Britain, for example, we read in a recent issue of the *Times Educational Supplement* (17th January 2003) that reception teachers are now having to work their way through no less than *3,510 boxes to tick*, as they are forced to assess every child against an absurd 117 criteria. A whole range of factors is continually reinforcing the cognitive 'hot-housing' atmosphere that pervades the education system – and which a number of eminent educationalists believe could well be doing untold harm to a generation of children. Yet a whole range of literature and research (some of it cited in the bibliography) is increasingly challenging the sanity of these trends; and the Hawthorn Press Early Years series is just one expression of a deep and widespread disquiet with the politicization of early years learning which has occurred with breathtaking rapidity – and with virtually no informed public debate – since the mid-1990s.

These trends are the tragic symptoms of a one-sidedly materialist, 'control-freak' culture which is laying waste to much of what we all instinctively know to be essential for living a wholesome, nourishing life. There is currently little if any empirical research being carried out on the medium- and long-term effects on children's overall social and emotional development of the soullessly mechanistic educational 'regimes' to which they are being unremittingly subjected. This is nothing short of a national scandal, at which future, more enlightened generations will surely look back aghast at our immaturity and almost wilful neglect of what really matters in living a healthy life. For anyone with even a modicum of awareness, the symptoms of a profound cultural alienation and malaise in children's lives are there for all to see.

Yet the 'modernizing' juggernaut simply ploughs relentlessly onwards, ignoring the mountain of countervailing evidence, and seemingly quite impervious to the insight that *its own policies and practices* are substantially contributing to this malaise.

One common effect of these disturbing trends – and this is a recurrent theme throughout the series, not least in Martin Large's new book – is what we might call *the dismembering of childhood*. It would be all too easy to despair and give up in the face of these modern trends; but as the books in the Early Years series compellingly demonstrate, there are tried and tested, viable alternatives to the aforementioned developments, grounded in a potent combination of perennial wisdom and cutting-edge research about child development, care, and learning. And there is a rapidly growing 'counter-cultural' public mood which is clamouring for a humane and demonstrably effective alternative to the deeply unsatisfactory fare currently on offer in mainstream culture.

The books in the Early Years series are holistic, informed, and practical – offering readers state-of-the-art information for those involved in early years settings (i.e. from birth to about 6 years), be they familial or professional. Later in this appendix, I will briefly review the books which have appeared in the series to date.

Some Symptoms of Childhood's Dismemberment

In today's 'hyper-modernized' world, the damaging pressures on young children are increasing. On BBC Radio 4's *Today* programme, for example, Anne Atkins recently described her routine experience of children *as young as three* being tested for entry into pre-schools. Little wonder, then, that the distorting effects of *anxiety* on healthy development and learning constitute a theme which recurs throughout the Early Years series. The crucial role of *free creative play* is emphasized by a number of series authors (Evans, Jenkinson, Oldfield, Rawson and Rose, Large): for as Professor Tina Bruce said to the Anna Freud Centenary Conference in November 1995, 'Play cannot be pinned down and turned into a product of measurable learning. This is because play is a process [which] enables a holistic kind of learning, rather than fragmented learning'. For Bruce, healthy childhood play naturally translates into adult creativity and resourcefulness.

Above all, the young child needs an *unintruded-upon space* in which to play with, elaborate, and work through her deepest wishes, anxieties, and unconscious fantasies. In turn, the child will thereby gain competence in healthily managing – with her own freely developed will – her curiosities and anxieties about human relationship and existence. Sally Jenkinson's seminal Early Years book, *The Genius of Play*, develops these arguments at much greater length than I am able to here.

Another recurrent theme in the Early Years series is the deforming effects on young children of *premature cognitive-intellectual development* – a significant theme, indeed, in Martin Large's new book. As already alluded to, a number of Western governments seem narrowly preoccupied with an over-intrusive, control-obsessed mentality – leading to a child 'hot-housing' ideology which may well be harming a whole generation of children, as even our own British Parliament's Education Select Committee has indicated. Sociologist Professor Nikolas Rose summed it up well when he wrote that 'Childhood is the most intensively governed sector of personal existence'.

We are already witnessing signs of the harm being done. A British National Health Foundation report found record levels of stress-related mental health problems in children. And the frightening scale of medically diagnosed child 'behavioural disorders' has recently been highlighted, with tens of thousands of schoolchildren with mild behaviour problems now being drugged with Ritalin – simply in order to control them. I believe there to be a demonstrable causal relationship between the burgeoning and comparatively recent epidemic in child 'behavioural disturbances', on the one hand, and recent early-years policy 'innovations' which demand an intrusive surveillance of children's developmental process, on the other – together with the imposition of premature, cognitive-intellectual learning at ever-earlier ages.

I believe that symptoms of so-called 'Attention Deficit Disorder' and the like are surely far better understood as children's *understandable* response to, and unwitting commentary on, technological culture's escalating over-stimulation – and not least, its one-sided distortions of early child development. Until our policy-makers develop the insight to recognize and then respond to this malaise at a political level rather than at an individualized medical level, the prevalence of children's 'behavioural difficulties' will inevitably continue to escalate – Ritalin or no Ritalin.

Re-membering Childhood: The Early Years Series

The principal focus of the Early Years series, then, is the promotion of healthy child development in its physical, emotional, and spiritual dimensions. The series is driven by the experience of parents themselves, rather than being primarily professionally or 'expert'-driven; and the distinctive approach represented in these books is strongly, but not exclusively, informed by the flourishing world-wide network of Steiner (Waldorf) Kindergartens, with their 80-odd years of accumulated wisdom on child development and learning.

The books offer sound information and effective practical input, based as they are on up-to-date research and practice. Hawthorn Press is working in close consultation with a range of parent educational organizations, and in this way the issues that the series is covering are emerging organically from the concerns of parents and educators themselves in today's demanding and complex world.

Future books are envisaged on such prescient issues as the importance of movement in early learning, parent and toddler groups, and holistic child development – among many others. The titles published to date are proving to be ideal study-texts for reading, study, and support groups, as well as authoritative sources on early years training courses. Many of the books promise to become *the* definitive works in their particular fields for years to come, and have already received very favourable reviews and widespread acclaim from a range of sources.

From *Helping Children Overcome Fear* …

A consideration of fear and grief in early childhood is a particularly apt focus for this, the first book in the series, for several reasons. First, *Helping Children Overcome Fear* demonstrates how the feeling life plays a crucial yet often neglected role in the young child's world. Fear and anxiety are certainly 'core' emotions which all children must learn to cope with and healthily manage; and Russell Evans provides us with an exemplary holistic approach to the child's emotional world in what can often be an exceptionally demanding and alien environment – that of professional medical care. Grief and loss are, moreover, central to human experience, and Jean Evans' work provides us with a wealth of insight into how these challenging emotions can be successfully worked with and integrated.

... via *The Genius of Play; Storytelling with Children;* and *Free to Learn* and *Ready to Learn* ...

Play and 'story' have traditionally been recognized as absolutely central accompaniments of a healthy well-rounded education – and Sally Jenkinson's *The Genius of Play* and Nancy Mellon's *Storytelling with Children* offer wonderfully inspiring testimonies to the importance of, respectively, play and story in child development. Research suggests that children deprived of stories in early life are statistically far more likely to grow up to possess anti-social tendencies; and there is compelling reason to believe that a similar fate might well await children who are significantly deprived of opportunities for creative, *unintruded-upon* play in early childhood (the High-Scope project in the USA certainly presents some suggestive corroborative evidence on this).

Steiner (Waldorf) education embodies both play and story in a comprehensive holistic framework which is developmentally attuned to the growing child in an explicit and fully theorized way. Lynne Oldfield's recent book *Free to Learn* ... represents the most comprehensive outline of Steiner (Waldorf) early childhood education currently available in the English language; and in the short time since its publication, it has already become *the* seminal text in this field – indispensable reading for all those seeking a viable, tried and tested alternative to the cognitive hot-housing mentality saturating mainstream early learning environments.

The most up-to-date research on learning and the brain is beginning to confirm the insights bequeathed to us by Rudolf Steiner, and upon which Martyn Rawson and Michael Rose substantially draw in their book *Ready to Learn* ... To take just one example, Steiner's indication to teach 'from the whole to the part' (rather than 'atomistically' from the part to the whole) is amply confirmed by neuro-psychologist Robert Ornstein, who writes that, in education, 'We should emphasize more of a top-down approach … first teaching the overall framework … We don't need a special right-brain learning program, but simply to put the large picture first in front of the student.' Rawson and Rose draw upon insights such as these to develop a systematic description of the main developmental processes involved in early learning and development, which in turn lay the essential foundation for later, more formal learning – or *school readiness*.

All in all, holistically inclined, genuinely balanced learning, along the lines outlined by Oldfield, and by Rawson and Rose, is arguably an absolute necessity for the future well-being of our species and our world.

… to *Set Free Childhood*

In writing this, the latest book in the Early Years series, Martin Large has performed a welcome service to those seeking a convincing rationale for reducing – or eliminating – the toxic 'screen culture' from their young children's lives. Large's impassioned, yet impeccably reasoned arguments challenging the ubiquitous screen culture are especially germane to the concerns outlined earlier. For my strong hunch is that if television and computers were removed from young children's everyday lives, the incidence of so-called 'deficit disorders' would decline. In other words, these so-called 'medical disorders' are *at least* as much symptoms of a deeply sick modern *culture* as they are symptoms of sick children … Yet what Large also makes clear is that we should not underestimate the vested commerical interests which wish to maintain and extend the toxic status quo: for what we needs must address in all this – and urgently – is *political, institutional, and centralized economic power*. To be blunt, if we fail to challenge and eventually to transcend these structures and processes, we will necessarily also be failing current and succeeding generations of children. This lethal cocktail, comprising a one-sidedly materialistic world-view and its associated powerful vested interests, certainly represents a formidable adversary to those who are determined to find better ways of raising our children.

Information Technology constitutes another highly contested issue within early years learning, and in British state-funded early years settings, a strong ITC presence is compulsory. Yet a wealth of empirical, anecdotal, and common-sense evidence – much of it reviewed in Martin Large's book – is unambiguously critical of this soul-less technology's impact on children – neurologically, psychologically, and socially. Certainly, we should be deeply concerned when we find eminent scientists like neurologist Professor Susan Greenfield of Oxford University suggesting that an increasingly ubiquitous Information Technology may entail profound long-term risks, including, as she writes, 'the potential loss of imagination, the inability to maintain a long attention span, the tendency to confuse fact with knowledge, and a homogenisation of an entire generation of minds'. 'These risks', she continues, '*could even actually change the physical workings of the brain*' (my emphasis). For anyone even remotely concerned about these possible effects, Martin Large's new book is quite simply indispensable reading.

Conclusion: Finding a Better Way

There is a growing sense that the tide is now turning against those pernicious cultural forces that have been systematically dismembering childhood – and towards a *re*-membering of a holistic, humanistic vision of childhood. To the extent that the Hawthorn Early Years series can buttress and reinforce this mounting sea-change in attitudes to childhood, it will have more than served its purpose.

The Early Years series is making available a rich range of books which will help parents defy the directives of modern culture (as

Neil Postman puts it), and *find a better way* to raise their children and help them realize their full potential. These books are helping parents and professionals alike to *reinvigorate* the art of *understanding children and their developmental needs.*

And above all, the authors in the series would all surely agree that education should nourish and facilitate, rather than subvert, children's innate *love of learning* for as neuro-psychologist Robert Ornstein has it: 'We're confronted with a large number of students and educators dissatisfied with the emphasis on drilling unrelated facts. Students [and children] lose interest, they don't see the relevance to their life ... We're trained for drills and learning things without connecting them to the world.'

Lastly, we invite you, the reader, to support this important series – and in so doing, to join the rapidly growing body of parents and educators who are determined to find a better way.

Richard House, Series Editor
Norwich, England
January 2003

Holistic Perspectives on Child Learning:
Some Further Reading

Baldwin Dancy, R. (2000) *You Are Your Child's First Teacher*, 2nd edn, Celestial Arts, Berkeley, Calif.

DeGrandpre, R. (2000) *Ritalin Nation: Rapid-Fire Culture and the Transformation of Human Consciousness*, W. W. Norton, New York

Elkind, D. (1981) *The Hurried Child: Growing Up Too Fast Too Soon*, Addison-Wesley, Reading, Mass.

Elkind, D. (1987) *Mis-education: Pre-schoolers at Risk*, A. A. Knopf, New York

Evans, R. (2000) *Helping Children to Overcome Fear: The Healing Power of Play*, Hawthorn Press, Stroud

Healy, J. M. (1990) *Endangered Minds: Why Children Don't Think and What We Can Do about It*, Touchstone/Simon & Schuster, New York

Healy, J. M. (1998) *Failure to Connect: How Computers Affect Our Children's Minds – for Better and Worse*, Simon & Schuster, New York

House, R. (2000) 'Psychology and early years learning: affirming the wisdom of Waldorf', *Steiner Education*, 34 (2), 10–16

House, R. (2001) 'Loving to learn', *Natural Parent*, May/June, pp. 38–40

House, R. (2003, forthcoming) *The Trouble with Education: Stress, Surveillance and Modernity*, Education Now Books, Nottingham

Jaffke, F. (2000) *Work and Play in Early Childhood*, Floris Books, Edinburgh

Jenkinson, S. (2001) *The Genius of Play: Celebrating the Spirit of Childhood*, Hawthorn Press, Stroud

Medved, M. and Medved, D. (1998) *Saving Childhood: Protecting Our Children from the National Assault on Innocence*, HarperCollins, Zondervan

Mellon, N. (2000) *Storytelling with Children*, Hawthorn Press, Stroud

Mills, D. and Mills, C. (1997) 'Britain's Early Years Disaster: Part 1 – The Findings', mimeograph

Moore, R. S. and Moore, D. N. (1975) *Better Late than Early: A New Approach to Your Child's Education*, Reader's Digest Press (Dutton), New York

Oldfield, L. (2001) *Free to Learn*, Hawthorn Press, Stroud

Paths of Learning (2002) Special issue on 'Spirituality in Education', issue 12 (Spring)

Patterson, B.J. and Bradley, P. (2000) *Beyond the Rainbow Bridge: Nurturing Our Children from Birth to Seven*, Michaelmas Press, Amesbury, Mass.

Postman, N. (1994) *The Disappearance of Childhood*, Vintage Books, New York

Prickett, S. and Erskine-Hill, P. (eds) (2002) *Education! Education! Education!: Managerial Ethics and the Law of Unintended Consequences*, Imprint Academic, Thorverton, Britain.

Rawson, M. and Rose, M. (2002) *Ready to Learn: From Birth to School Readiness*, Hawthorn Press, Stroud

Salter, J. (1987) *The Incarnating Child*, Hawthorn Press, Stroud

Sanders, B. (1995) *A is for Ox: The Collapse of Literacy and the Rise of Violence in an Electronic Age*, Vintage Books, New York

Schweinhart, L.J. and WEIKART, D. P. (1997) *Lasting Differences: The High/Scope Preschool Curriculum Comparison Study through Age 23*, High/Scope Press, Ypsilanti, MI; Monographs of the High/Scope Educational Research Foundation No. 12

Steiner Education (2000) Special Issue: 'Caring for Childhood: Waldorf and the Early Years Debate', Vol. 34, No. 2

Thomson, J. B. *et al.* (1994) *Natural Childhood: A Practical Guide to the First Seven Years*, Gaia Books, London

Getting in touch with Hawthorn Press

We would be delighted to receive your feedback on Set Free Childhood, how you handle the electronic media in your own family, tips for coping, health advice, alternative activities, useful research - so that this can be considered for incorporation into future editions.

Visit our website for details of the Education and Early Years Series and books for parents, plus forthcoming books and events, at www.hawthornpress.com.

Ordering Books

If you have difficulty ordering Hawthorn Press books from a bookshop, you can order direct from:

United Kingdom

Booksource Distribution
32 Finlas Street, Glasgow G22 5DU
Tel: 08702 402182 Fax: 0141 557 0189
E-mail: orders@booksource.net
Website: www.booksource.net

North America

Anthroposophic Press c/o Books International
PO Box 960, Herndon, VA 201 72-0960
Toll-free order line: 800 856 8664
Toll-free fax line: 800 277 9747

Dear Reader

If you wish to follow up your reading of this book, please tick the boxes as appropriate, fill in your name and address and return to Hawthorn Press:

☐ Please send me a catalogue of other Hawthorn Press books.

☐ Please send me details of Early Years events and courses.

Questions I have about the Early Years are:

_____

_____

_____

_____

Name _____

Address _____

_____

_____

Postcode _____ Tel. no. _____

Please return to: Hawthorn Press, Hawthorn House,
1 Lansdown Lane, Stroud, Glos. GL5 1BJ, UK
or Fax (01453) 751138

SFC